REVIEWS

"Reminiscent of the work of Brene Brown, *Fear Less* is rich in vulnerability and authenticity. The chapters in this book provide actionable tools and steps to help us face that which is holding us back. This book lit a fire within me and had me asking, what am I truly afraid of? And what will it cost me if I don't face my fears?"

-Alisha Higgins | Public Speaker
and Co-Founder of G.L.O.W.
Gals Learning Our Worth

"When I first heard about just the *conception* of *Fear Less*, I knew it would be something I needed to read. How right I was, and it didn't disappoint. From the opening lines, to each and every chapter, to the final acknowledgments, this beautiful book will inspire, empower and challenge you. You will laugh out loud, and you will definitely shed some tears. You will want to buy copies for your girlfriends, sisters and moms--do it! This gem is something every woman needs to read."

-Rebecca Voros | Author, Speaker,
and Founder of the Ignite Women's
Conference Series and Bold
Abundance Coaching

TRANSFORMING FEAR INTO COURAGE WITHIN
RELATIONSHIPS, CAREER, SOCIETY, AND SELF

FEAR

LESS

AN ANTHOLOGY

CHRISTINE ESOVOLOFF | KRISTEN THOMPSON | SHARON HUGHES-GEEKIE
ANGELIKA MCKEEN | ESTEE ROE | ANDREA KELLY | REBECCA JUETTEN
LISA POZNIKOFF | MICHELLE B. VAZQUEZ | KRISTY KEUS
LORENE HUGHES | HAILY KORTEKAAS | LISA KERN | BETSY GRINDER

CONTENTS

FEAR OF FAILURE AND SUCCESS

Preface

Christine Esovoloff

"I'm not afraid of storms, for I'm learning how to sail my ship."

-Louisa May Alcott

When the idea behind this book first percolated in our minds, we were completely unaware of how timely the subject would become. Enter the global pandemic of COVID-19, the subsequent economic fallout, and the civil unrest we would experience, and fear seems to be at the forefront of all of our minds. And, while it might present differently for everyone— as anger, indifference, hatred, anxiety, activism, etc.—the bottom line is, underneath it all lies fear.

When we started discussing the content, we intended it to focus on smaller, "hold you back from living your best life" fears. The "I want to ask for a promotion but I fear rejection or success" type of stuff. But, over the eighteen-month production of this book, what we realized is that it doesn't matter whether we are facing a global economic crisis, or a new job interview, the fear we experience is imminent. Real or imagined, big or small, fear is fear: A biochemical response to a perceived threat. And while fear has many negative connotations, it is incredibly important. One of the most primitive and basic emotions spanning countless species, fear is a warning that something or someone may be dangerous. It keeps us alive, keeps us safe, and it keeps us from making terrible decisions. Fear has been, and continues to be, imperative to our survival.

It is ironic, and perhaps nature's cruel joke, that our brains react the same, whether we are faced with a threat to our life or faced with a job interview (or whatever your trigger might be). Whether actually dangerous or not, it registers the same;

we fight, flight, or freeze. It seems fear holds us back just as much as it keeps us safe.

The bottom line is, fear is natural, normal, and even crucial . . . but it needs to be kept in check.

The tricky part, and one that became very apparent to me while writing my chapter for this book, is that it is much easier to develop an unreasonable fear than it is to get over it. We develop narratives around past experiences and traumas that very much pave the way for us moving forward. Oftentimes, as was the case for me, we may not even be aware of the story we are perpetuating.

Perhaps we self-sabotage an employment opportunity because we unknowingly fear success. Maybe we exhaust ourselves trying to balance work and home life because we are terrified of letting people down. Or maybe we go through our relationships never letting anyone in because we are scared of intimacy or abandonment.

We all have these stories, and whether we are aware of them or not, they hold us back. And while it is completely natural to feel fearful when approaching something new or uncertain (in fact, it is biology), many of these fears are not keeping us safe at all—they are keeping us stuck. They are getting in the way of the life we want and deserve.

When I look back on all the opportunities I have turned down, relationships I have destroyed, and excuses I have made, every single one of them was rooted in fear.

Fear of abandonment.
Fear of intimacy.
Fear of being vulnerable.
Fear of failure.
Fear of rejection.

And although these fears felt so real, and still do sometimes . . . they just aren't true.

Our first title for this book was *Fear is a Liar*, simply because it so often is. Fear tells us we can't, that we shouldn't, that we are not enough, and that we aren't deserving. Fear fills

8

our heads and our hearts with untruths. We ended up deciding to change the title a little later after coming to the realization that overcoming fear is not a linear process. Sometimes,
we don't overcome it at all. Sometimes, we just learn how to
quiet the whispers in our head, how to power through anyway,
how to *Fear Less*.

Nelson Mandela once said, "I learned that courage was
not the absence of fear, but the triumph over it. The brave man
is not he who does not feel afraid, but he who conquers that
fear." The stories in this book are ones of just that—of feeling
afraid, and moving forward anyway. They are stories of courage, of triumph, of strength, and of grit.

This book will inspire you to not only acknowledge your
fear, but to start leaning into it—letting your fear live with you,
not for you. These stories speak of overcoming childhood misconceptions of how family should be, bullying, people pleasing, aging, relationships, work expectations, and so much
more. Whether we are faced with rejection, abandonment,
heartbreak, or trauma, the connection within these pages is
that we must acknowledge fear and run with it, not from it.

FEAR

WITHIN RELATIONSHIPS

"I believe that every single event in life happens in an opportunity to choose love over fear."

-Oprah Winfrey

FEATURING:

HAILY KORTEKAAS
LISA KERN
ANGELIKA MCKEEN
BETSY GRINDER
CHRISTINE ESOVOLOFF

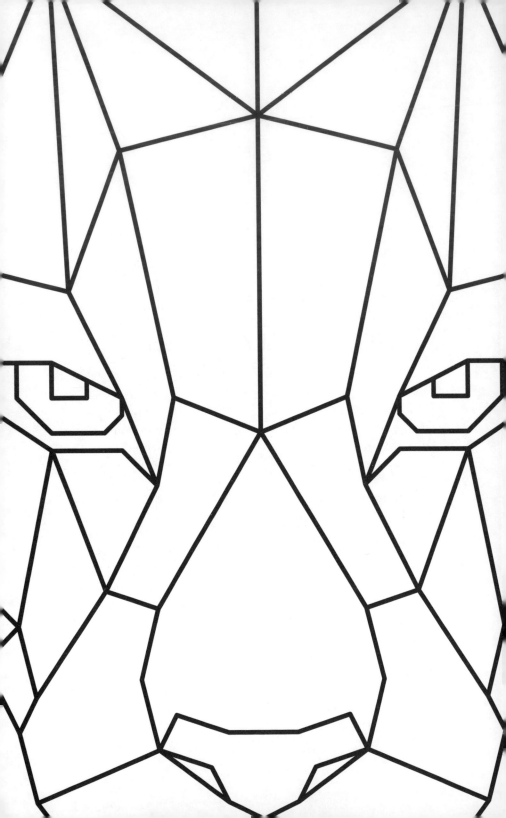

From the moment we come into the world, we crave connection. In fact, we are dependent upon it. As babies and young children, our ability to thrive, learn, and grow is determined by how loved and safe we feel. Our well-being and even our neurological development, hinges almost entirely on the adults we have in our lives—our caregivers. They are the first people who teach us about vulnerability, trust, love, and self-efficacy. We learn how to perceive the world, how to feel about ourselves, and how to manage stress, by watching them.

As a mother, this has caused me a great deal of guilt. When I watch my kids struggle with trepidation or anxiety, I can't help but wonder what I could have done differently, what I could have changed to better support their well-being. Similarly, when I reflect upon my childhood, I can recognize some moments that were pivotal to my developing story. The moments that taught me that it wasn't safe to speak up or that I was better off playing small. They were often small incidents, but they taught me to keep my walls up and remain guarded; since relationships were risky, they were unsafe. Whether we had a fantastic childhood or a challenging one, the subtle messages we received paved the way for our relationships moving forward. And oftentimes, without even realizing, the patterns we developed in childhood continue to impact us for years into adulthood. From being ultra-independant or a chronic people-pleaser, to struggling with fear of abandonment or vulnerability, these coping tools and patterns get in the way of our success.

Facing our fears around relationships is no easy task, but it can be one of the most rewarding experiences along a personal growth journey. When we open our hearts and heal our wounds, we give permission for others to do the same—to heal. And when we love, trust, and have compassion for ourselves, we stop tolerating anything less from the people in our lives. When we build our connections on authenticity, acceptance, boundaries, and forgiveness, it opens up the space for everyone to thrive.

My hope is that the next few chapters in this book shine a light on the relationships in your life where fear might be holding you back, or where you might be playing small. Allow these stories to ignite a belief inside you—a knowing that you are enough, and that the world needs you to spread your wings.

CHAPTER ONE

Uncovering the Root of Fear

"Too often we forget to ask a
crucial question that would help shift
our lives for the better:
Why am I afraid?"

Haily Kortekaas

www.hailykcoaching.com

ig: @hailykcoaching
fb group: Enlighten + Expand: Spiritualpreneurs

Haily Kortekaas

Haily Kortekaas is a life and business coach helping women face their fears, connect to their intuition, and uncover a purpose that is true to themselves and their dreams. Her biggest accomplishment was finally facing her own fear and finding the courage to follow her own calling to write and teach. She lives in Ottawa, Ontario with her boyfriend and two cats and in her free time she enjoys reading, writing, yoga, and spending time with friends.

W e as humans like to ask why. *Why did this happen to me? Why did you do that? Why isn't this the way I thought it would be? Why am I not happy?* Among all of these whys, we forget to ask a crucial question that would help shift our lives for the better: *Why am I afraid?*

Too often people take their fears as a given, believing that because fear is present, there is legitimacy to it and sound reasoning behind it. I believe that until each of us takes the time to question our fear, and face it with courage, it will continue to haunt us. Its persistence will show up in each area of our lives, leading us further into unhappiness.

We resist fear, attempt to ignore it, and numb out the discomfort, because it triggers something unpleasant inside us. What's worse, our egos, the part of our brain operating to keep us safe, will use our deepest wounds to keep the fear alive.

In many coaching sessions, my clients want to know how they can tell if they are making a decision that is good for them, or making a decision based out of fear. One way to recognize if fear is driving your decision-making is if you notice unpleasant patterns appearing in your life. Patterns such as attracting a particular personality type in friends and colleagues, being turned down for promotions at work, or just feeling the overwhelming sensation that you are stuck. It's especially frustrating if you believe you've been doing your best to avoid such circumstances from happening, but they continue to happen all the same. In these situations, it is a fear, or a commonly accepted negative belief that is recreating the pattern on repeat.

Using my life as an example, when it came to romantic relationships, I was attracted to men that couldn't love me the way I felt that I wanted to be loved. Each time another relationship ended I felt lost and confused. Why was this happening over and over again? I blamed them, I blamed my parents for not loving me enough and passing down their negative relationship habits, and I blamed my body for not being pretty and lovable enough. It feels easiest to blame someone or something else for the results that are ultimately caused by choosing fear in our lives. I wasn't ready back then to see the real problem—the fear and the negative habits that were holding me back from attracting what it was I really wanted.

So if it's fear that is creating an outcome that we don't want, then why does it exist? Why can't we just let it go and make all of our dreams come true?

No matter where you are in your life, fears are guaranteed to come up. We all have an ego, that when triggered, elicits the fear response in an attempt to protect us. It is the natural human response to danger. We choose to listen to our ego when we sense danger, often taught to us by other people. Maybe you were taught by your parents all of the many dangers you need to worry about. Maybe you went through a traumatizing experience in your life. Maybe you have cultivated a need for control and it has become your first response to the unknown. Whatever your fear may be, if you have learned to trust and put your faith in your fear over listening to your heart it's time to consider why.

How can we understand our fear?

In business school, we are taught that before trying to solve a problem it is most important to get to the root of it. One way to do this is to continue to ask yourself *why?* I find it is most helpful to jot my answers down on paper to see the progression of your thoughts and how they have led you to the particular results you are now noticing.

- Upon recognizing that a fearful thought has come up, ask yourself: *Why do I feel afraid?*
- When an answer surfaces, ask again: *Why do I feel this way? Why does that matter?* Or, *Why is it important to me?*

UNCOVERING THE ROOT OF FEAR

- Continue asking yourself five or six times until you feel you've hit the mark. You'll know when you feel a dead end or an "aha" moment. Then ask one last time: *Why do I feel this way?*

In my experience, delving deeper and deeper into the fear will eventually bring the underlying truth of your fear to light, so that it can be healed. What's even more surprising is that the core fear, the one that has eluded you, is often totally unrelated to the original fear that you began to question. Fears can stem from a buried memory or a false representation of something that had happened to you as a child. Or it can come from somewhere completely unrelated, warped by ego and life experiences. Fears can morph themselves into a monster that haunts your mind, causing you to continue to make decisions because you didn't know to question it.

Here is what happened when I applied this method to a fear relating to my relationships. For years I had this recurring fear over the idea of being trapped, whether in a job, or in a commitment of some kind. Without realizing it, it also came up as resistance to being trapped in a marriage. In my twenties, this seemed like a reasonable enough fear. I was young and wanted to explore all life had to offer. Consciously though, I knew that getting married was something that I wanted to do—eventually. So, as I got older the fear didn't align with what I felt I wanted, and as my friends began to get married, it started to become less and less reasonable. In an effort to ignore this fear, my mind had convinced me that it was the result of the emotional upsets and disputes that took place inside of the marriages I witnessed growing up. My ego would show me a mirage of images of my parents and other couples whose fighting and disagreements caused tension and disharmony. I was reminded that marriage would keep me stuck in these types of situations, believing that divorce wasn't even an option.

The difficulty we face as adults is that because our childhood mentality didn't have the capacity to understand the world fully, any misconceptions we perceived back then became our worldly "truths". And until we question those misconceptions, it will continue to be the lens through which we view the world. My ego latched onto these images as a truth of marriage that must be avoided at all costs.

As I started to learn more about the ego and the ways in which it tries to keep us *safe* (for me, safe meant single), I realized that maybe marriage wasn't what I was terrified of after all. People fight, so what? Is this really what I'm afraid of? My ego then turned my attention to the men from my past, those who had hurt me and weren't able to give me the love that I felt I needed. I figured I wasn't lovable enough to attract the type of love that I wanted and deserved. As I began to realize this was also a false childhood idea, and concluded that none of those men were the one I was meant to marry, I had to ask myself, *what if I ended up being with the right person*? Would this fear still be valid? Here is the really scary part—my ego couldn't counter anymore. The fear was still there, and I still didn't know why . . .

This is a tough spot to be in; it's where some people might get stuck, feeling like they are failing. I took the ego's flotation devices away and it didn't know what to do.

This was when I had to be okay with being in a state of confusion. This is the time for surrender.

I reached a point in my mid-twenties where I thought I had *made it*. I had a master's degree, a job with a good salary and a pension, and was living in one of my favorite parts of the city with my serious boyfriend, but . . . I was miserable. I had accomplished what I had set out to do so why wasn't I happy? Why did I work so hard to get here only to realize that it wasn't what I wanted at all? This was a hard truth that I had to face, and soon after the revelation that the life I was living was not the life I wanted, it quickly took a 180, and everything fell apart.

"We are all broken,
that's how the light gets in."
–Unknown

It took that relationship—the one I thought would be *it* for me—to take a good hard look at my beliefs about partnership. In leaving it, I had to reassess my valued *work hard* ethic in relation to creating the life I wanted. I was working so hard for something that wasn't meant for me and I finally had to open up and surrender to the fact that I wasn't happy for a reason. I had to learn to trust that this all happened *for* me, not *to* me, and that there was a new life waiting for me on the other side.

This is what happens when we begin to let go.

Changing our fears will ask us to change our life. It's a time when we are being asked to have faith and hold the possibility of a positive future. It was at this point I realized that I was tired of my old ways of thinking and being. When would the hard work bring me happiness? How was it that other people were living their reality of a loving relationship? Why was I choosing men that I didn't really want to be with? This situation, yet again, was reinforcing my old fear of being trapped. I thought I had gotten to the root of it, but being alone and frustrated, I had no choice but to question it further. This time I really had to surrender, and once I did, the answers came in surprising ways.

In 2020, during the COVID-19 global pandemic that forced so many of us to stay home, I had plenty of time for self-reflection. It was at this point, after a year of focusing on me, I found myself in a more healthy, stable relationship with an amazing man. I felt like I was finally connecting to the joy and happiness that eluded me for so long. Self-care goes a long way to creating the amount of self-love I needed to take the next steps in my journey. I was ready to finally ask myself, *Why am I still afraid to take the next step? Why am I afraid of being trapped by commitment?*

The answer came to me in a book called *It Didn't Start With You* by Mark Wolynn. The basis of the book is the idea that there may be fears, doubts, blocks, frustrations, and negative energy that was biologically passed down from our parents, grandparents, and even possibly generations before them. He tells many stories of individuals that come to him completely

unsure and unaware of the reasons behind their irrational behavior, claiming that it is "something outside of themselves."

I found further confirmation in this idea while reading
Will I be Enough? by Karyl McBride when she quotes Alice
Miller stating, *"Traumata stored in the brain but denied by our
conscious minds will always be visited in the next generation."*

This opened me up to the possibility that maybe this fear
really didn't start with me. It was oddly comforting for me to
think that maybe I had finally found a solution. That perhaps
I was only carrying the resulting trauma, so that I can heal it
and prevent it from moving down into future generations.

In his book, Wolynn suggests a very similar approach of
digging for answers. He provides a variety of tools and exercises that allow you to dig deeper into your fear. And so I did.

I started by asking my family members about the history
of women feeling *trapped* in my family. The evidence was
undeniable. Through generations, my grandmothers and great-
grandmothers had no choice but to get married, meaning
that they had to give up on their personal dreams and goals.
My great-grandmother was impregnated during the war and
forced to leave her home country. My grandmother became
pregnant at a young age, forcing her to give up on her dream
of going to school and getting an education. I was told other
similar stories of women through generations feeling trapped
and limited by family responsibility.

I have coached with many women who also hold this belief deep in their core, fearing the guilt of not putting their husband and children's needs first; they feel that somehow they
are a bad mother, partner, or wife. While this fear that I had
made sense, its prominence in my life forced me to question
it. Is it really true? Does it have to be the way I choose to live
my life?

It might feel easy to blame men, societal norms of past
generations, or those people today who are still living in fear
for the problems of current times. However, any type of trauma is shared by all of us. The belief and expectation that being
married and having a family means that women can't be their
own person, have their own dreams, goals, and desires outside

of family life is something that we change if we are willing to face our fears and heal.

Fear is not something that is meant to be ignored, resisted, and drowned out with distractions, it is our responsibility to have courage and face it. To have the willingness to question it reveals what is at the heart of it.

I might not be able to go back into history and relive it, but I can live my life now. I can take everything I learned and stand up for what I believe to be true. The combination of fear from the past and negative beliefs about myself was keeping me stuck in ways I couldn't comprehend all of those years ago. I began to believe that there was something wrong with me, that I wasn't meant to have all the things I wanted. If this is where you are, then get curious. Ask for guidance, or a mentor that can help you. Moving through fear takes courage, but you don't have to do it alone. It is liberating when you can cultivate the ability to know when to ask for help. I couldn't have done it without books, courses and especially the help and guidance of some pretty amazing women that have counseled and coached me on my journey.

To end this chapter I'd like to note that the men I've run away from have found their paths, and many of them are living happily in their own way. They were guides on my journey. There is no point in looking back and regretting the decisions we could have made if we didn't feel any fear. We could wonder how our lives would have been different if it wasn't ruled by fear, and yet, fear can sometimes bring us to our own path as well. If I had felt no fear I wouldn't have been called to write this chapter and to coach women with similar struggles. Fear is not an ugly monster to be avoided, it's a sign—calling you out and pointing to an area of your life that currently needs more love and attention from you. Have compassion for yourself as you navigate this. If you can dig deep enough, you can find the strength you need to push forward into a new realm of endless possibilities.

CHAPTER TWO

PERSPECTIVES FROM A RECOVERING PEOPLE PLEASER

"When you gain approval of the only person that really matters, yourself, you will find the truest path to health and happiness."

Lisa Kern

www.healthyholistichappy.com

ig: @holistic_ot | fb: @Lisa Kern

Lisa Kern

Lisa Kern is an eternal optimist with an open mind and heart. Her spectrum of interests runs wide, and she has a deep-rooted belief that you should follow your heart and intuition at all costs.

She considers herself a student of life with a passion for personal development, health, and wellness.

Lisa has a master's degree in occupational therapy with a bachelor's in science from American International College. She spent ten years of her career as an OT specializing in neurological rehab before she decided to follow her passion and true purpose of empowering others to live their healthiest and happiest as a health and wellness coach. She is now focused on building a brand to empower others to optimize their healing from the inside out—addressing body, mind, and soul.

As a multi-passionate entrepreneur, Lisa also holds certifications as a brain injury specialist, yoga instructor, reiki practitioner, and is co-founder of Work Your M.O.T.O.R., an online home exercise program for stroke survivors.

Lisa is married and lives in Massachusetts with her two children, Will and Gavin. Skilled at seeing the silver lining in situations, Lisa's personal mantra is, "Without struggle, you will never know your strength."

On a journey of personal development and still trying to figure out who I was in my thirties, I threw myself into the teachings of Stephen Covey who famously wrote *The 7 Habits of Highly Successful People*. One of the habits is to "begin with the end in mind." The exercise is to visualize that you are attending your own funeral three years from today. Think of who is attending, what your legacy is, who you impacted, and if you lived a fulfilled life. Heavy, right?

Beginning with the end in mind was the catalyst for me to start living a life without my constant companion: fear. I asked myself these questions: *Do I have a legacy? What do I stand for? What am I passionate about?* You see, I am a recovering people pleaser with engrained characteristics and a certain way of thinking from my childhood; being quiet was a positive trait, being submissive was preferred, and being the best was the only way to get recognition. One day, I realized that in living to please other people, somewhere along the line, I lost myself. Craving belonging and approval in my younger years, I became a master at agreeing, blending in, and stuffing away difficult feelings, so I could be a *good* girl; the result was an adulthood of fear—fear of conflict, fear of rejection, and fear of abandonment.

Are you a people pleaser? Have you ever let fear of speaking up or being rejected stop you in your tracks? People pleasing is a cute-sounding name for an addictive behavior pattern where you feel controlled by your need to receive approval from others and make them happy. People pleasers hide their true feelings and are skilled at avoiding difficult emotions at all costs; they become a chameleon to blend in with their crowd and be welcomed. With the belief that being nice will protect them from rejection, people with these tendencies find it hard to say no and measure their worth by what they can offer to others. Oftentimes, there is a history of emotional neglect during childhood. It is also common that they were given the message that to receive love they had to be of service. People pleasers sacrifice their own wants and submit to the needs of others—all in the effort to receive the recognition they yearn for.

THE STORY

When I was a child, I developed a learned behavior to stay quiet, play small, and keep peace in the house. Although my father had many wonderful qualities, he was an alcoholic with a short temper. I also had a troubled brother that was proficient at testing boundaries and pushing the wrong buttons. Additionally, the women in my life all seemed to be drawn to a certain type of man; alcoholics with short fuses. Through their examples, I learned that to keep a "partner" content, you had to walk on eggshells—at all costs, do not anger them. If you were unsuccessful, you were the reason they drank, causing them to yell and scream, to turn red in the face, which only drove them to drink more. It was a vicious circle that I learned to avoid. There was no point in arguing because conversations in our house were one-sided; obey the rules or get screamed at. It was an easy lesson, so I learned to not speak up. I wore my conflict avoidance badge proudly and earned my love by being quiet.

I remember a time when my older brother got in trouble, yet again. After being berated by my father, my mother had heard enough and tried to stick up for him. It took a lot for her to use her voice and put my father in his place, but when she did . . . she was a force to be reckoned with and transformed into my hero. This, of course, sent my father into a tailspin, calling my brother a string of expletives and awful names. He threatened my mother with an ultimatum; my brother had to move out, or my dad would. Tears streamed down her face. I wanted desperately to be by her side, but I was paralyzed by fear and hid in my room. My brother had been shuffled around before going to Georgia to live with my aunt who was a former marine, sent to "scared straight" camps in hopes that he would see what his future would be if he didn't change, but my mom was done shuffling. She firmly stood her ground and let my dad walk out. I remember pleading. I remember my father already being so drunk that at the young age of eight, I knew he wouldn't be able to drive safely. I came out of my room and threw myself at his feet as he had one hand on the door. I feverishly tried to unlace his boots and convince him to stay. If he would only take his boots off, everything would be okay. My dad wore work boots because he was a long-distance trucker. He would be gone for days at a time, before cell phones and FaceTime, so I wouldn't see him for long stretches. I always looked forward to helping him unlace those boots because once they were off, it meant he was home, he never went back out after the boots were off. It was my favorite thing to do, unweaving the figure eights in a rhythm with both hands and feeling the leather strings unwind. He would always pretend as though he couldn't do it himself and I felt so important. This time, he didn't let me near his boots and he slammed the door in my face. He was gone. I tried to speak up against his choice and actions, and yet it made him leave. My mother, I'm sure, consoled me; maybe we watched TV, had ice cream, or read books. I remember that we were both so worried about him that she later woke me up so we could drive around town looking for his little green Volkswagen Rabbit. It was at the second bar we drove by; the dark, dingy kind of bar with no windows that reeks of cigarettes and piss. The kind of place where you go to drink alone and tell the bartender your woes. *Well, at least we knew where he was.* We circled around the parking lot and went home. Hours later I was woken up by him falling up the stairs. Yes, up the stairs. He luckily drove home on autopilot, but was too drunk to put one foot in front of the other. When my mom kindly escorted him in, I ran out to the kitchen to see that my father had pissed himself—the whole right side of his Levi jeans were soaking wet. My eight-year-old brain learned a lesson that was false, but engrained. Speaking up makes people angry. Angry people drink so much they piss themselves. Note to my little self: Don't endanger your father by making him so mad he goes out drinking. Don't speak up.

THE LIE

That is only one story of so many instances where speaking up led to heartbreaking rejection and abandonment. Of course at the time I didn't see what was happening, but it's so clear now, that this is where my lack of courage comes from. I was conditioned over so many of these scenarios that speaking up leads to explosive fighting. I rarely saw a disagreement get resolved through calm conversation where both parties were heard. This pattern stuck with me as a teenager and adult, especially with men; it's why I couldn't speak up. I had sex when I didn't want to, I stayed with people long after the relationship ended, and I apologized when I didn't do anything wrong. I let the lump that formed in my throat when I got nervous choke me quiet when I should have spoken up for things I believed in. I didn't ask for a raise when I knew I was overqualified and underpaid. The story on repeat in my head was that my voice didn't matter and speaking up equaled conflict. Too many times I settled when I should have had the confidence to say that I deserved more.

THE HEALING

As I write this next part, my ego—my inner critic, my mean girl voice, whatever you want to call that judgmental FEAR that holds you back—is shouting loud and clear, *Who are you to be giving advice on speaking up?!* I'm quieting her and reminding myself that if someone can benefit from these steps, it's worth sharing; I believe that you teach the things you need to learn the most.

These were the action steps that were helpful for me to gain confidence, to give fewer fucks, and quiet the fear of speaking up.

Step 1: Find the Root Cause

As well as having a strained relationship with my father, whose motto was "My way or the highway," my mom passed away when I was fourteen-years-old. That crappy age where you need the most love, guidance, and support. With high school starting two months later, I made up my mind that I wouldn't be the sad girl. Being a freshman would be hard enough and I refused to be known as the girl whose mom died. I pretended like it didn't happen and I never talked about it. Bottling up my emotions seemed like a safer bet because, remember, I had a father that didn't "do" emotions. So, I stacked my school schedule, excelled at sports, and got high grades. As long as I can remember, I always worked two jobs and had an active social life. It *never* dawned on me that I was keeping busy so I never had to sit alone with my thoughts . . . I said yes to everyone and everything, so I didn't cause problems and no one would think I was sad or a burden. In my messed up little mind, fear told me that being sad was being weak.

Can you relate to this? Have you found yourself overextending, over performing, getting straight As, being a perfectionist, or holding yourself to ridiculously high standards only to prove to someone else that you are worthy?

When I finally recognized where this fear was rooted, I was able to accept it and start to do the necessary work to undo this false belief that my voice was not important. This step is freaking hard, and you might need help from a trained therapist to ask the right questions, but believe me, it's necessary.

Step 2: Know the Difference Between Being *Nice* and Being *Kind*

Being nice is about being liked by others and monitoring your actions so you come off in a pleasing manner. It's making sure you don't cause any hurt feelings, upset, sadness, fear, or anger to another person. It's the thought process that tells you that if you don't ruffle any feathers, people will like you and give you approval.

Being kind, on the other hand, is being real and truthful. You can speak up for yourself, be assertive, share your opinions and ideas in a caring and generous way, however, the desire is to be helpful instead of being liked.

Niceness is rooted in fear, and kindness is rooted in love. As a reminder, it's OKAY to not be nice all the time!

Step 3: Learn to Set Boundaries

For a true people pleaser, this step can be very hard. It is a skill to say no and it will take time to break your automatic habit of saying yes. Repetition of a pattern can create new pathways in your brain and will eventually come as second nature. But, if you are not used to saying no, this can be a daunting task. Practice by coming up with a catchphrase like, "I'd love to, but I can't" or "I might have a conflict. I'll check and get back to you." Don't offer an explanation or reason why. You are entitled to politely decline. It is estimated that it takes three to six months for a new behavior to become a habit. Therefore, the more you practice this technique, the more successful and confident you will be when it's needed. Boundaries are essential to healthy relationships and flexing your voice muscle. In order to set proper boundaries, you need to know what your limits are. What are you willing to do or tolerate? This is the new you we are talking about, not the old people pleasing one. Set clear boundaries, practice being assertive, and be mindful of your feelings when you get a gut reaction. If it's not a "Hell Yes," then strongly consider making it a "Hell No."

Step 4: Take Care of You

Self-Care 101 teaches that you can't pour from an empty cup. If you are similar to other people pleasers, you likely put your needs behind those of everyone else. It seems obvious that we should take care of ourselves first before we are fully capable of taking care of others; however, if you happen to fall into the category of busy working mom, it's incredibly hard to do all the things, all the time. This results in feeling guilty about finding time to do the little, yet important things that keep us sane, happy, and healthy.

Start by making a list of how you want to feel, look, and act. What does the highest version of you look like? How does she talk to people? How does she dress? Now visualize this version of yourself being confident, brave, attractive, and magnetic to others. Repeat affirmations that you are capable of being this version of you. Talk to yourself like you would to your best friend. Take pride in your mental health, alone time, and appearance. Do this as a form of self-love, not vanity and not for anyone else. If it feels forced at first, fake it till you make it! Start to believe you are worthy of your time and schedule self-care into your routine.

Examples of Self-Care (in case it's been so long you don't know what you need!)

- *Physical Self-Care*: Quality sleep, stretching, walking, yoga, cardio or weights, eating healthy foods, resting when you need it.
- *Emotional Self-Care*: Creating boundaries, asking for help, meditating, cuddling and hugging, journaling, creative tasks like drawing, coloring, cooking, singing.
- *Sensory Self-Care*: Book a massage, walk barefoot in the grass, sit by the fireplace, listen to music, bask in the sun, cuddle a furry pet.
- *Mental Self-Care*: Unplug from technology, read a book, do a craft, learn something new, talk to a friend, declutter your home.
- *Social Self Care*: Have a phone date, host a game night, write a card and mail it, spend time with people that uplift you, not drain you.
- *Spiritual Self-Care*: Spend time in nature, do a random act of kindness, meditate, pray, do yoga, listen to your intuition, let go of negative attachments.

Step 5: Do the Inner Work

The last (and hardest) step is to commit to doing the inner work. For me, this happened when I started having physical manifestations of my emotional wounds. Although in my late twenties I could check all the boxes: married to a great guy, two kids, a dog, house, career, wonderful friends—I had this nagging feeling that something was missing. Gradually, I was getting short-tempered and my moods were changing. I started suffering from severe panic attacks. They would happen randomly while I was doing the dishes, driving home from work, or playing a game with my kids. Nothing specific seemed to bring them on. Each time though, my throat felt like it was closing, my heart would audibly pound in my ears to the point where I couldn't hear anything else, and on my chest felt like a thousand-pound weight was crushing my sternum. Also, without reason, I was pushing my husband away, and I was suddenly completely unfulfilled and sad. It's worth mentioning that during this time frame, I got recurrent bronchitis, laryngitis, had a dry chronic cough, and got tested for thyroid disease because I always felt like there was a lump in my throat. *Sometimes you have to slow down instead of speed up.* What I needed was a release of the pressure that I felt from society to "do it all." Like many women, I was conditioned to pile on more instead of taking a time out. From here, I found a fantastic naturopathic doctor, bit the bullet and saw a psychologist, and I also worked with an energy healer who did several sessions of reiki on me. No surprise, I had a block in my throat chakra from my years of suppressed emotions and inability to communicate my wants and needs.

Listen to your body. It will usually whisper to you before it yells. Find someone that can support you and think outside the box in terms of health care. I saw my primary doctor several times without any explanations of my symptoms and never any mention of how my emotions could have been affecting my physical health. Be your own advocate. No one knows your body better than you.

THE MESSAGE

When you hold back and keep parts of your true self unattainable from fear of rejection, or not being liked, you will never feel truly loved because *no one knows the real you.* When you gain approval of the only person that really matters, yourself, you will find the truest path to health and happiness.

I hope you feel empowered to let go of the fear, call it a liar, and quiet that voice in your head that tells you your opinion or desires don't matter. Because they do! Everything you want is on the other side of fear.

References:

Braiker, Harriet B. *The Disease to Please*. New York: Mc-Graw-Hill, 2001.

Hani, Julie. "The Neuroscience of Behavior Change." *Start-Up Health*. August 8, 2017. https://healthtransformer.co/the-neuroscience-of-behavior-change-bcb567fa83c1.

CHAPTER THREE

FEEL THE FEAR, BUT DON'T GIVE UP THE WHEEL

"To shift your current reality, be it mental or physical, you need to brace yourself for intense feelings of discomfort; change is a necessary part of growth."

Angelika McKeen

www.angelikamckeen.com | www.trunaturalist.com

ig: @ang_mckeen | @trunaturalist
fb: @AngMcKeen | @trunaturalist

Angelika McKeen

Angelika McKeen is living her rural dream just outside of Waterford, Ontario, in a home she designed and built together with her husband Karl; her two sons, two cats, and one dog make up her family unit. Angelika is driven in pursuit of a meaningful life and her many passions, which include the study of languages, horticulture, animals, and most creative projects. She completed a double major in English and Japanese studies with a minor in French at McMaster University.

Angelika ended her corporate career as a general manager for a national hotel management company when she became a mother and has since moved on to become a real estate agent. She is entrepreneurial at heart and is currently putting some of her many ideas into motion, including starting a venture of her own.

I always hated the feeling of fear: the flushed skin, the sickening feeling in my stomach. Maybe it was because I experienced such extreme levels of fear growing up that I began avoiding it at all costs. Living in a constant state of anxiety in childhood will do that to you, I'm sure. Being the eldest, I already had a lot of expectations and responsibilities, but being uprooted and moved to three different countries, growing up with an abusive father, and living a rather unsheltered existence in subsidized housing and on welfare all required me to grow up rather quickly and become more resilient, at least on the outside. I worked really hard to become absent of fear. In reality, I believe I simply did a good job of ignoring it in order to be able to move forward and escape my childhood. I was often described as strong, independent, capable, self-sufficient, someone who doesn't need anyone or anything. Looking back now, I'm not surprised I turned out that way.

I share my story reluctantly. Another result of my childhood trauma was the need to deny its existence because for a long time I believed that (like fear) acknowledging it would give it life. However, over time I have come to realize that it's important to do quite the opposite. So I'm making an effort and sharing my experience as yet another step in my journey to overcome my fear.

Step One: Acknowledge Your Fear

On the surface, my father was a charming Eastern European man. At least that's how most people saw him. But my family and I saw a much different version. He was a true con man in every way: a compulsive liar who manipulated people without remorse. In fact, he was so good at working things in his favor that at the age of nineteen he was able to escape

45

communist Poland without a passport, gain citizenship in Sweden, and ultimately open his own semi-legitimate business. I say "semi-legitimate" because he didn't always conduct his affairs above board. He would often surround himself with people of dubious character, and there were many instances of his cheating others.

To the average person, my father would portray himself as a jolly man who loved social settings and reveled in showing off his amazing family; he dragged us most places to help his image, and we were expected to do our part. To us, however, he was a monster. He was extremely verbally and emotionally abusive, and at times even physically abusive with my mom. He kicked my half-brother out of the house at the age of seventeen merely for being an inconvenience—this meant that shortly after gaining access into Canada, my brother was left to fend for himself in a new country without language or skills. He had only moved in with us three years prior when we were still in Sweden, and for a while he took the brunt of my father's abuse. However, once he was no longer in the picture, I became the eldest child again at ten years old. It didn't matter what I did; if I even looked at my father wrong, I would receive his uncontrollable anger. He would berate me so relentlessly that I often ended up curled up in a corner, crying uncontrollably, unable to take a breath. One of my earliest childhood memories is of my mother attempting to come to my aid, only to have my father turn on her and reduce her soul to nothing. I walked on eggshells most of my childhood, fearing my father's next blow-up.

My dreadful experience during these early years was amplified by the fact that we moved to Canada and I became an immigrant. Imagine a child who is already very anxious because of an abusive father and now add the discomfort of not being able to speak the local language. I was obviously uncomfortable socially, which made me seem weird to some and an easy target for others—this also came with a healthy dose of bullying. I had all the right elements to create the most gut-wrenching discomfort. Making friends seemed impossible; being alone and retreating inward became my normal. As a result, fear became a subconscious driver in my life. I avoided anything that would put me in an uncomfortable position, and I worked hard to stay ahead of it.

I chose to—or rather, had to—move out when I was seventeen to get away from my father. And so, I decided to move in with my boyfriend. This didn't seem like a bad decision at the time, but it ended up being a very unhealthy relationship that I endured for thirteen years (we even married). I chose this path most likely out of my fear of being alone or just not knowing any better. I still didn't have a lot of friends, so I immersed myself in school and work. Luckily, I never had a fear of working hard: if anything, it was a good distraction and something I could control, so I always put in the time and effort to make something of myself. I went to university and even worked three jobs at one time. I decided to major in English because I had had enough of feeling uncomfortable in Canada. I took what I thought was a temporary job in hospitality; however, it became my career as I ended up climbing the corporate ladder. The thing is, any time a more meaningful opportunity would present itself, I would find a reason not to pursue it. My passions often drew me to jobs that included language teaching, usually abroad; at one point, I was one step away from moving to New Zealand, but I ended up convincing myself that travelling was a far-fetched notion. I still struggled with my communication in English, so one failed interview would usually be enough for me to abandon everything.

Fear prevented me from taking those big-moment opportunities: the life-changing, the transitional, and the impactful steps towards my passions. It kept me from those decisions that would develop my skills and lead me closer to my real purpose on this planet.

Fear was in the driver's seat; I made my decisions based on misplaced notions of success and a need for a sense of security. Since this was my priority, I never focused on getting to know myself, always choosing to run towards something seemingly secure, to take the *safe* route, the one with least contention. I had the motivation and the drive, but I lacked the *heart* to pursue more exciting things if they meant making significant changes.

I wish I knew then what I know now: that any worthwhile pursuit forces significant change. How else are we meant to grow? At the time, though, the *unknown* caused tremendous discomfort because I couldn't control the end result and because failure was not an option. This was one of the biggest hurdles I needed to overcome, or rather, one I needed to let go.

Step Two: Confront and Question Your Fear

Eventually, my life—the one I created through careful decisions and manifested unintentionally through my fear—had become extremely *uncomfortable*. I was in a toxic and abusive marriage, working a job that demanded attention twenty-four hours a day, and barely had a relationship with my family and my few friends. I'm not sure what it was exactly that eventually put things into perspective for me, but I imagine it may have been the little steps I had started taking towards pursuing some of my own interests in an effort to create more balance in my life. These included various creative classes, reading, yoga, and hiking. By this time, I had worked my way up to being a manager for a top-branded hotel chain. I was finally making good money and got to travel (even if it was for work), and I started to feel good about what I had achieved.

Seeing glimpses of myself happy in those spaces began to show me how unhappy I was in my day-to-day. That's when I seriously started contemplating divorce and moving back home; at the time, I thought there was no way I could handle the debt we accumulated over the years, so moving home seemed like my only option. However, my mother was still with my father, which would make such a move very uncomfortable. They also lived five hours away, meaning I would most likely have to leave my job.

All the scenarios spinning in my head were overwhelming, as any drastic change would take me into an unknown (uncontrollable) future. Fear, again, showing up as confusion, doubt, and worry about anything that would require going out of my comfort zone. In this sense, I think it's important to distinguish legitimate fear, which stems from actual danger or bad decisions, and the fear that comes from a place of insecurity or inexperience. I had many *false* fears to get over, but the biggest ones were those of loneliness, regret, and failure.

Step Three: Dare to be Brave

To shift your current reality, be it mental or physical, you need to brace yourself for intense feelings of discomfort; change is a necessary part of growth. In the end, trying to expertly fashion and organize my life, even though I had worked hard at it, could only take me so far. That's because worthwhile opportunities, and often the most valuable experiences, appear spontaneously and take you out of your comfort zone. I've come to realize now the reason these moments evoke feelings of discomfort is because deep down within your soul, you know you are supposed to seize them. When I finally decided to divorce, it was like I hopped on a rollercoaster I couldn't get off, or better yet, a high-speed train that wreaked havoc along the way. My divorce wasn't pretty, it didn't follow a plan, and if I were to describe the actual series of events, you would most likely get whiplash trying to keep up. I was overwhelmed with all the emotions involved with breaking off a thirteen-year relationship with someone who didn't want to let me go, and being scared to follow through with it; depression, anxiety, and self-destructive behavior began to unfold. I was making poor decisions in my social life—dating terribly, drinking a lot, taking drugs—and I was just about ready to quit my job.

By complete luck (or divine intervention), my work offered me a promotion; a new management position had opened up closer to my family. I took the opportunity and moved back in with my parents. Things were very different this time around. My mother was now able to stand up to my father because the kids were grown and she was working full-time—she could support herself. My father had a change of attitude, knowing that my mother had the means and could leave him at any moment.

I eventually managed to move out and put the pieces of my life back together, and my mother, maybe seeing light in my experience, ended up divorcing my father after thirty-two years of misery: proof that your life is not static and your reality can change. Out of all the kids (myself and my five siblings), only one sister still speaks to my father on occasion. He continues to be elusive, telling lies meant to divert us from what he's really doing or where he really is.

Even though everything seemed to be flipped on its head, my life felt like it was headed in the right direction. However, the question I was asking myself now was: *How do I make sure not to repeat the same mistakes—somehow unconsciously lead myself down the same road?* I think indecision is a common by-product of fear because it clouds your ability to listen to yourself and what you truly want; instead you're concerned with everyone and everything else outside of you.

Step Four: Truly Know Yourself

It became quite clear that I needed to do some self-discovery. I finally had the freedom to design my life again, but I was questioning everything. *Would my decisions make me happy? Were my choices just playing it safe?* I don't remember where I got the idea, but I began to journal, listing things I wanted in my life, traits and skills I wanted to develop. I thought that maybe this would keep me on track, focus my attention on the road ahead, and keep me from getting derailed again by fear. There are many books and coaches that specialize on the subject of building self-confidence. The important thing is to start the search for yourself. Getting a clear vision of who you are, what you believe, and who you want to become is an integral step to take you where you want to go. In the beginning, it wasn't easy to dig up exactly what I wanted out of life. I needed to reconnect with myself and reset without the influence of years of programming and self-preservation. This took time. I took random workshops that piqued my interest and connected with nature by taking walks through the forest, starting a garden, and surrounding myself with houseplants. By just following your interests, you will eventually open doors to reveal who you really are; you only need to take those first, small steps.

Even though I have become more confident in my decisions, I am by no means completely fearless. I know fear can never truly be absent. Fear is elusive and can shape our life, our motives, and the choices we make. For this reason, I think it's important to ask yourself whether the choices you are making are really what's best for you or whether you are just playing it safe. Are you living your desired life or are you just surviving?

My childhood experience set the stage for fear in a big way. For a long time, I lived in a survival mode, and so my fear ended up running the show in an attempt to keep my head above water. My instinctual response was to do what I felt I needed to protect myself. However, once we're aware of what our fear can look like and how it shows up within us, it becomes easier to face. I know fear has shown up when I can't stop questioning myself or my actions; it's as if my spirit is yelling at me when I'm struggling with an important choice. A wise friend once told me, "Fear wouldn't show up unless it was really important." Meaning, if it didn't matter, you wouldn't think twice about it. Pay close attention to these moments.

Fear is a part of us, whether we want it or not. Even if you are an ambitious, hard-working, and seemingly confident individual, you could still be operating from a place of fear. Fear has become a companion I try to get to know well. I continue to use my journal often to work through my thoughts, which can be chaotic and often difficult to interpret, but much clearer once I put them on paper. I no longer run from my fear or react to it. Instead I listen and try to understand it.

Living fearlessly doesn't mean you are without fear, but rather learning to recognize the role it plays in your life and, in turn, not allowing it to control you.

CHAPTER FOUR

FOUR-LETTER WORDS

"It also was a great reminder that healing takes time—it was ugly at times, and this still hurt."

Betsy L. Grinder

www.giventothegrinders.com
ig: @BetsyLynn
fb: @GiventotheGrinders | @YourDailyServing

Betsy L. Grinder

Betsy Grinder is a small-town girl with big dreams. Married at twenty-four, Betsy knew she wanted a family and couldn't wait to start a life with her husband, Aaron. The life she dreamed of shifted and it took some time for her to look at her situation as anything other than heartbreaking. Betsy changed her way of thinking, living, and loving; she opened up her mind and heart to what a beautiful life really looks like. With a home full of pets and a sweet husband by her side, she now sees that her life is the way it was supposed to be all along. Her newly-started business is now serving her community in ways she never knew possible and her happiness is not measured by anything or anyone but herself.

G rowing up in the early '90s as a female seems like a different life than the one we are living now. Looking back, life seemed simpler, actions seemed a little slower, emotions weren't at an all-time high, and fear wasn't felt nearly as much. When I was nine years old, fear was what I felt running home after dark from my friend's house six doors down. I remember calling my parents from the landline, insisting my dad meet me in the driveway—just in case. Now, walking after dark is something I do for relaxation.

That same year when I feared running home, my parents were in the middle of a divorce. Not a nasty, hateful divorce. Not a divorce that scars you for life. It wasn't messy, it was civil. It was filled with love and us children were put first. I consider my brother and I to have been some of the lucky ones. This was when relationships became so important to me. Looking back, this is why I love the way I love: effortlessly, fully, recklessly, and always giving it my all. This is the way I feel all of my emotions. My parents are still friends to this day; holidays are not split and everyone sits at the same dinner table. I still consider us the lucky ones.

The '90s were about finding out who we were as a family, but also as individuals. My parents supported all of our ideas—letting us get dirty and learn the hard way, all while welcoming us home at night with open arms and a warm heart. We were taught life lessons like how to hook your own worm, throw a softball, burn cookies, and love unconditionally. We were also taught that it was okay to feel your emotions, all of them. I also think this is where those reckless feelings come from. Your emotions were yours and time spent dealing with them was time well spent. Reflecting on my upbringing, it's no wonder I have always wanted to pass along this reckless love and passion for life that was given to me.

When I was in middle school, I started to notice more about myself and my surroundings. My short temper, obsession with even numbers, and need to fit in. I fell into the role of a teenage girl in a small town by wearing football jerseys on Fridays and sitting in the same seat every day at lunchtime. This season in life shapes you, makes you strong, and creates memories to carry with you. This stage in life was also hard for me: I was told I had a benign brain tumor. Although we were relieved that the tumor was not cancerous, the list of side effects was extensive and included a lifelong battle with hormone imbalance. I was allowed to sit with my fear of this illness; my parents gave me the space and time I needed and with that came the strength to overcome those difficult feelings. I was not going to let this negatively affect my life or hold me back. Being told at the age of fourteen that conceiving children might be a struggle was not bad news at the time—now, the news haunts me.

At twenty-one, I met my now-husband. His love for me is something I never knew was possible. He matched my reckless emotions and overcame any emotion with me, for me. Telling him the news I received when I was fourteen was a struggle for me, but for him, trials and tribulations are looked at with a steady heart and calm mind. Fear was something he may have felt for a minute, but he did not let it take over his life. In the same way my family had done when I was younger, he can feel an emotion, process it, and move forward. Soak that up, folks. Know this is possible for you as well.

We slowly and steadily took on the news of possibly never having children of our own—we were able to remain calm throughout the months of appointments, heartache, and hope, accompanied by long drives and countless medicine bottles. We thought we'd hit rock bottom, but then we felt a glimpse of hope as our dream came true—I became pregnant. Aaron knew before me; he said he could see a difference in me. We finally caught a break in this four-year journey. Sadly, in October of 2017, I miscarried. I never thought I could feel such pain and failure. I took time, a lot of time, to work through the emotions that came with such an event. We decided to take a break from the appointments, the long drives, all the medications, and we never looked back.

As much as I would love to tell you I left the emotions of that season of my life in the past, I have not. I have had hard days where the pain feels like it happened yesterday. I have had days full of hope and feeling like we could start this all over again . . . but then fear creeps back in. The fear of falling on the floor, overcome with disappointment and pain. The fear of sharing how I was doing with others all over again. The fear of failing as a wife, as a mother. The fear of possibly not wanting what I once wanted so badly. That last fear stunned me.

I started writing down what it was like trying to conceive and then having a miscarriage. I was working through how it felt to be someone who wanted something so badly but could not have it. I started a blog and this helped me feel less alone and initiated the task of healing. It also was a great reminder that healing takes time—it was ugly at times, and still hurts to this day.

Throughout the years, my sweet husband was always supportive and would kiss my forehead and tell me it would be okay; two kisses, of course, because my obsession with even numbers didn't end in middle school. It was to the point that I insisted on even numbers for our T.V. volume, the number of ice cubes in my drink, and the number of pillows on the couch. To some, this little act was silly, but to me, numbers have always been important. I frequently saw number combinations on our way to doctor's appointments and would Google them as soon as we hit the waiting room. I would realize that the trips from point A to point B had been forty-four miles, or that it was four miles to the nearest rest stop. I couldn't let this go; four was meaningful to me then and still is today. There is power in numbers and how we see them. I took a drive down the numerology trail and loved what I found. Seeing a repetitive combination of fours is considered a sign that you need to remember your roots and where you came from. For me four meant to be patient, trusting and loyal to the process. What a great reminder to look back at the years that shaped me as a person, the lessons learned, and the important relationships I had.

As I worked through my pain, I remembered that my preferred relationship when I was younger was one where I was needed. I found myself looking for someone to need me, to depend on me. Surprisingly, that wasn't hard to find. I joined boards, volunteered my time, and felt joy in being needed. I was needed for Monday meetings at 4 p.m., and Tuesday dinner meetings, and again for Thursday recaps, and then Saturday morning events. These distractions were welcomed to keep my mind and heart busy while my friends caught up to where I was in life: married, starting families, and announcing it all on social media. If you have worn the "ttc" or pregnancy loss shoes, then you know there's no sting quite like a pregnancy announcement online. This pushed me further into working with my community. I fell in love with serving my town and helping others—I never knew this passion inside of me existed. I'm thankful for the path that got me there and the doors it opened along the way. But there were still doors in our home that were left closed, like the nursery we had once put together; the crib was now a great spot for my sweater collection and picture frames. The years of pouring myself into others left my cup empty and the healing process paused. My time spent at home with the ones I love the most was at a minimum. To be honest, being home hurt some nights; walking past rooms and spaces I had other plans for was a hurtful reminder of my pain and the feeling of failure rose to the front of my mind. *Was I failing at the one thing I promised my husband? Was I failing as a wife and, even worse, as a woman?*

The constant reminder of who I was not and of how far I was from who I thought I would be at this point in my life forced me to dig deep. I no longer wanted to be "Betsy, who was trying to start a family," or "Betsy, who will put together this event." But who did I want to be? Aren't these questions we all face? Where are we supposed to be? Who are we supposed to be?

Who we are is not measured by wealth, babies, jobs, or hours spent volunteering. It is about how we treat ourselves. Toss those expectations others have of you to the side! This life you are living is for you and the future you are creating and working towards is only going to be made by you. The months leading up to my new found peace were filled with reading all the self-help books, long sweat sessions at the gym, alone time with God, and telling myself I was enough. Telling myself that where I am is a good place and that who I am surrounded by mattered. I removed my community board sash and spent more nights at home with my family—a family that consisted of three loving, loyal dogs, a stinky cat we rescued, and a two-hundred-pound mini pig. Yes, another sign I married a good one. My husband let me walk into our house with a pig that I promised would stay small forever. Boy, was I wrong. All of them loved me and were happy to see me, but not as happy as my husband. He still loved me the same as he did that day on the beach more than six years ago when we vowed to be together forever. His love for me did not dwindle with my feelings of failure; it did not dissipate when the medicine bottles did. *Thank you, Auron.*

My life was no longer run by fear—an awful four-letter word that I let take over my being. I let go of the feelings of not being enough and of self-doubt. I once again became more self-aware and my numbers were appearing daily. Yes, the fours were back and I was happy to see them along with other number combinations. Similar to seeing a cardinal on a bad day, knowing your loved one in Heaven is there with you, these combinations were a reassurance that I was heading in the correct direction. For years, I saw the numbers two, three, and two again. This happened at the strangest times, not when I would see the fours, but when I least expected it. The numbers appeared on my mileage, or the time of day, or even the page of a book I was reading. I gave these numbers no power or recognition until, for months straight, they were everywhere. "That's it," I said out loud to myself as I headed to my bookshelf. "Twos and threes are not for me." When numbers are brought to your attention over and over it is considered a sign, or that you have a specific message coming your way. This combination signifies relationships, spirituality, and your creative self. It also symbolizes optimism, compassion, social interaction, and inspiration. Clearly, I had yet another shift coming. As if looking at myself in this new light wasn't enough, something more was on its way.

Although I was no longer serving on every community board I could, I still had a passion for my town and the many people in it. I took what I had been seeing into perspective and—it hit me while I was drying my hair, as most of my ideas do—something clicked. What if I take my passion for serving others, my years of being in the food service industry, and everyone's love-language—food—and combine them all? No fear was felt when I put this together; not many doubts were had when I put my idea out there; and, it hasn't slowed down since. I started a meal service that delivers healthy dinner options to people in my city. This business came together just as the COVID pandemic hit and we were ordered to stay at home. Those numbers were on my side. I am fulfilled by this business because it nurtures my love for others. I am met with smiling faces as I deliver fresh, healthy meals to customers and then wave to them from a safe distance outside of their homes. I am sometimes the only person they see all day and I cherish our time together, even if it's just a quick conversation. I have built relationships with many of my customers—they pray for me, we trade books, and write notes. I am needed. I am also present and happy and I'm known as "Betsy, just Betsy."

Four-letter words such as fear can run our lives, only if we let them. I look back at where I was when this all started and where I was within myself. I am not there anymore and you aren't there either. The four-letter words I use to describe myself now are able, true, and bold. Some words that I used to get to where I am now were love, cope, feel, and pray—lots of prayers. These powerful words hold such meaning in our lives and how you use them is up to you.

CHAPTER FIVE

RE-WRITING MY STORY

"I am writing a story where despite what happens from chapter to chapter, the ending is always the same—I am enough."

Christine Esovoloff

www.christineesovoloff.home.blog

ig: @the_ginger_journal | fb: @christine.ginger.journal

Christine Esovoloff

Christine Esovoloff is a published author, speaker, marketing executive, and owner of *The Ginger Journal* blog. In a word, she is a storyteller. She has had a passion for writing and entertaining people since she was old enough to hold a pen. Often compared to Princess Merida for her fiery mane, Christine is definitely *Brave*—approaching life with humor, gratitude, and of course, a healthy dose of sarcasm. Her journey has taught her that the biggest hurdle to success is almost always fear, and that accountability and empathy are key ingredients when it comes to achieving our dreams.

Despite the many hats she wears, if asked what her favorite role in life is, she will tell you it is being a mom. Christine resides in the sunny Okanagan Valley, British Columbia, with her kids, fiancé, and dog, and loves the amazing lakes, mountains, and wineries all at her fingertips. When she is not busy with writing, work, or family, you can usually find her hiking, sipping some delicious Okanagan wine, or getting bendy in a hot yoga class.

F ear has gotten in my way for as long as I can remember; from being terrified of failure in elementary school gym class (because sports weren't exactly my jam), to not pursuing the career I wanted because I *just knew* that I would fail. Whether it was success, rejection, failure, loss, or change, I've been scared of it all. And although I am fully aware that fear is something that every single person on the planet experiences, I have often wondered if maybe I am just a little weaker than most people. You see, fear has done a pretty darn good job of getting in my way and mucking stuff up for me. I liken it to some sort of schoolyard bully, stomping around and shoving my innocent dreams into mud puddles, while I stand on the sidelines, watching like some sort of helpless spectator. Shaking my head and muttering, "Such a shame, that one had potential." It wasn't until my divorce that I realized how bad it was and started to tackle my fear with any level of intention. In fact, most of my thirties have been dedicated to sorting through and dealing with the negative messages and ideas I've accumulated over my thirty-nine years on this planet.

I thought I was doing well. I wouldn't say I was arrogant so much as I was feeling very confident that I was getting on top of things; I considered myself to be fairly self-aware, as well as a big believer in taking ownership of my life. So, when it came to calling myself out on my crap and changing my patterns, I felt like I was doing a decent job. Being gentle with myself and forgiving of others, while holding myself accountable, and keeping the "pity parties" to a minimum. To be honest, I was rocking the whole self-improvement thing.

Or . . . so I thought.

Life has a funny way of keeping you humble. In retrospect, I probably needed a little reality check. As it turns out, while I *was* doing a decent job of "unpacking my crap," I was also spending most of my time on the "fluffier," easier to manage items, while completely ignoring the uglier, bigger picture stuff that probably should have taken precedence.

Apparently, despite my self-awareness and willingness to face yucky feelings, I (like a lot of people) had a pile of crap that I was just plain ol' avoiding. Like the junk drawer in my kitchen, I just pretended it wasn't there. It was ugly and overwhelming; I just kept shoving more stuff in it and slamming it closed. I suppose I figured that I could get to it later? Or perhaps I thought I could just keep it tucked away? I mean, as long as its contents can be kept hidden, it's not really a big deal, right?

Wrong. Very big deal. Turns out, it is the quiet, seemingly harmless junk drawers in our brains that can be the most destructive, and mine was jam-packed with all sorts of juicy things that were, unbeknownst to me, completely affecting every aspect of my life.

The brutal reality that I was not, in fact, an enlightened self-improvement warrior, but rather, a big messy ball of denial, resentment, and shame hit me one day as I was listening to a podcast in my car. The podcast was focused on fear and as I was listening to the host discuss her struggles around fear in relationships, I found myself feeling more and more uneasy. There was this heaviness in my chest, one that appeared to be screaming, *Hey lady! Pay attention. There is something you need to learn here!*

I have always excelled at relationships, even during the most troubled parts in my life, even before my enlightened self-improvement warrior stage when I was drowning my sorrows in poor decisions and questionable men. I have always made friends easily. I can get along with almost anyone. I am loving, kind, and easygoing.

So, what the hell was with this pit in my stomach?! What was bugging me so much about what this podcast host was saying?

I turned off the podcast, drove home, and did what I normally do when I am faced with something unpleasant: stew in a pit of misery for a while. Although I always strive to be accountable for my emotions and to keep any "pity parties" to a minimum, I am also a firm believer that in order to work through your feelings, you have to actually let yourself feel them first. And apparently, there was a lot to feel on this particular occasion.

I'd love to tell you this "pity party" was short-lived and I got to the bottom of my feelings rather quickly, but let's just say I sat on my couch long enough to make it through two seasons on Netflix, and drank an amount of wine that I am too embarrassed to share. (Nothing will show you that you have a little more work to do in terms of practicing healthy coping skills quite like being abruptly faced with unresolved trauma.)

Apparently, the junk drawer I had avoided for so long contained a crapload of stuff from my childhood (surprise, surprise). It's not like I wasn't aware that I had a bit of a unique upbringing, but I had been in denial about how much it had impacted me, particularly in terms of relationships.

I was an only child, and raised by a single mother. My mom was an elementary school teacher in her late-twenties. And my father was a divorced man in his mid-fifties. There was talk that I might have been the product of an affair, but it was never really clear. Whether it was my father's age, my mom's career, or the fact that I was the result of a casual fling, neither of my parents felt prepared for the old "and baby makes three" situation that they were facing. So much so that they thought it would be best if no one found out, I was put up for adoption, and they could just go about their lives.

My father, blessed with the ability to just walk away, did just that, leaving my poor mother to hide her swollen belly behind baggy sweaters and give birth to me alone, and in secrecy. I don't know much about what that time was like for her, but as someone who has had two kids, I cannot imagine how stressful and painful that was for her. After I was born, I was immediately put into foster care to await my adoption, and my mom, after a long nine months, was finally able to go on with her life. That is, until three weeks later, when she changed her mind and promptly turned around to come and get me. What can I say . . . I was cute as a button.

Although my mom decided to keep me, her life wasn't easy. She struggled silently (as so many do) with mental illness and shame, all while single parenting and working full-time.

For the first ten years, she coped quite well, but was often dissociative and emotionally unavailable. Her mental health continued to deteriorate over the years and she eventually turned to alcohol to numb her pain.

My mom passed away four years ago, in 2016, and it has been quite the process to write about her most vulnerable and painful times. A part of me wanted to protect her and only speak of the sunny times, while the other wanted to be honest about my childhood. Shame and fear thrive in secrecy, so the decision to share our story comes from knowing that neither of us, particularly my brilliant mother, deserves to feel ashamed about our journey together.

I learned from a very young age that it is important to ensure you are not left by other people. That you must prepare for the worst-case scenario, but do everything you can to avoid it. From being unwanted during pregnancy, or left in foster care at birth, to being rejected by my father (he never did come around), or having to demand attention from my struggling mother—I extracted from those experiences that I could be rejected or abandoned at any time. I coped in the best way I knew how, which was to become exactly what everyone needed me to be—the charmer, the sweetheart, the jokester, the relatable one, the agreeable one.

The ultimate chameleon. *What are your thoughts on politics? I can totally see that perspective! Your favorite foods? Music? Mine too!*

I learned the delicate dance of quickly evaluating what was needed of me in any given situation. And when I fucked it up (because even Oscar-winning actors don't nail every role), I would be flooded with shame and fear and prepare to be left all over again.

I think the biggest shock, and the greatest (most unpleasant) realization, was that, although I seemed to thrive in relationships, and although I was aware that I often acted like a bit of an emotional chameleon . . . the one thing I hadn't been aware of was how badly I held everyone at a distance; I had never let anyone fully in and was always somewhat preparing for them to leave. In fact, I have always had one foot out the door. Sure, I am loving and warm, but if I get the inkling that you might leave, or if I feel too vulnerable, I will run. I will push you away. I will self-destruct. I grieved your loss before we even met.

The truth is, I hadn't been thriving in relationships at all. I had been surviving. I had continued to manage my relationships in adulthood as I had as a child—in fear. Fear of not being enough. Fear of being rejected. Fear of being left. And the fear of being vulnerable.

Now, the irony of this whole situation is not lost on me. Here we have a girl that craved nothing more than belonging and connection and so she responded in the most rational way she knew how, which was to hide who she truly was and run in the opposite direction of belonging and connection.

I'm not going to lie, I have had moments of wishing this stayed in the junk drawer.

The crux of the matter is, I feared being seen for who I truly was. I saw myself as awkward, quirky, unintelligent, and unremarkable. I had taught myself that who I was was not good enough. So I forced myself to become someone else, so that people would love me, stay with me, accept me.

Let me tell you, discovering that I was: a) not a relationship champ as I had originally thought, and b) had subconsciously avoided any true chance of connection by hiding any and all authenticity, hit me hard. Perhaps I had been unaware of my fear around relationships because I didn't want to be aware of it. Maybe I hadn't been ready to face the abandonment and rejection I had experienced in my childhood. Maybe that wound had been too deep to look at until just recently. It really doesn't matter. What matters is what I choose to do moving forward. Keep hiding, or step out of the shadows and into a new way of being. As tempted as I was to stay on that couch with a bottle of wine, night after night, I wanted to show up differently in my relationships. I wanted to be vulnerable, I wanted true connection, even if it meant risking getting hurt.

There have been times where it felt like a fight, where everything in my body is screaming at me to not speak up, to not rock the boat, to stay where it is safe. But I have learned, by staying the course, and by being myself, that I actually open up space for my relationships to become so much richer.

Turns out, people appreciate authenticity.

The risk of getting hurt is always there, no amount of hiding who I am can change that. In fact, it often makes it worse. And the little girl who is so full of fear is still very much inside of me, but I can be gentle with her now, coaxing her out, one step at a time.

Opening myself up in my relationships hasn't been easy—it is an adjustment for everyone. And I know that combating the deep-rooted lie, *I am not enough*, that I have held onto for so long will likely be a long battle, maybe even lifelong. But, so far, it has proven to be worth it. I don't run anymore when it gets scary. I lean in now, even when things are uncomfortable. I have hard conversations, I tell people when they have hurt me, and even more difficult . . . I listen when they tell me that I have hurt them.

I am learning, slowly, that I am enough. Even though I am flawed, even though I am wounded, even though I still have a junk drawer full of stuff to deal with, I am enough. I don't need to hide anymore. I don't need to try to control everything. And I don't need to be what I think everyone else needs me to be.

Deep down, it often still feels like I am opening myself up to be hurt again. That by letting people in, I risk them leaving me again later. But I know that this is just an old story that I have been playing on repeat for far too long. The stories we tell ourselves are often untrue.

Besides, I'm writing a new one now. One where the beauty of vulnerability and connection far outweighs the risk of fear or getting hurt; where I am safe in all scenarios because I trust myself, where I can be a self-improvement warrior and a work in progress all at the same time.

I am writing a story where despite what happens from chapter to chapter, the ending is always the same—I am enough.

FEAR

WITHIN SELF

"Fear and self-doubt have always been the greatest enemies of human potential."

-Brian Tracy

FEATURING:

ANDREA KELLY
LORENE HUGHES
REBECCA JUETTEN
SHARON HUGHES-GEEKIE
LISA POZNIKOFF

"**S**he is her own worst enemy." This is an expression I have heard time and time again, but I hadn't given it much thought until recently. The expression implies that, in our lives, we are not victims of circumstance but participants as well. It indicates that we often get in our own way or hold ourselves back when it comes to going after life goals. It suggests that we are accountable.

Accountability can be uncomfortable. It often feels easier to hide behind excuses and blame or to practice avoidance. Admitting that we play a role in our own undoing can be painful, as it means facing old wounds and, often, confronting lifelong fears. Exploring our inner dialogue, as well as the narrative that we have built our lives around, takes courage. And deciding to turn inward and explore the areas in which we hold ourselves back isn't easy. But neither is the alternative. Living a life dictated by fear and doubt leads to stagnation. It prevents us from moving forward. Giving ourselves the opportunity to see the areas of our lives in which we are our worst enemy also gives us the freedom to make a change—to choose something different. When I came face to face with the narrative I was holding on to, I found that it was filled with self-doubt.

I can't.
I shouldn't.
I am not smart enough, pretty enough, talented enough, thin enough, young enough, rich enough . . .

And behind all of that doubt, of course, was fear.

Stepping away from the excuses I was making, the blame I was putting on others, or the avoidant behavior I was practicing did not happen overnight. In fact, these are still patterns I need to be aware of. As with tackling any bad habit developed over a lifetime, the shifts are not instantaneous. It takes commitment, perseverance, honesty, and determination.

But when we choose to dive deep and unearth the narratives that we have made into our mantras, we open ourselves up to a beautiful opportunity—a chance to step into our power and create a new story, one based on possibility, courage, and hope.

These next few chapters are just that: they are stories of discovery, of tackling our inner fear and doubt, and of reaching for courage even when we are still filled with uncertainty.

May these chapters inspire us to face the doubt and fear that we have been carrying and encourage us to create a new story for ourselves. A new story where, fear may still be present, but it will no longer be the loudest voice in our heads.

Chapter Six

Fear is a Teacher

"When I removed the eating disorder, the substance abuse, the habit of wanting to disassociate, I was choosing to embrace life in the most authentic way and suddenly life showed up for me."

Andrea Kelly

www.yourbestbeing.com | www.tapintoyourmagic.com
anchor.fm/yourbestbeing

ig: @andreakellylove | fb: @yourbestbeing
li: Your Best Being

Andrea Kelly

Andrea Kelly is a transformational coach and writer with an academic background in business and over a decade-long career in real estate project sales. Andrea discovered her passion for self-development after struggling silently with an eating disorder for over twenty years. It was her healing journey that propelled her towards her passion for personal growth and become a certified hypnotherapist and transformational coach. She is guided by her mission to help others remove their personal blocks and transform their lives to become the best version of themselves. Andrea resides in beautiful Kelowna, British Columbia, Canada where she enjoys spending time creating, writing, hiking, and being by the water.

I n the midst of our fears, struggles, and worries, there are gifts to be received, lessons to be learned, and a life to be lived. Although it can be easy to coward away from the feeling of fear, as I did for many years, the opportunity to walk through its fog can, and will, take a person into the depths of a more vibrant existence. Fear takes on its own shape for each one of us; at the same time, many similarities can be drawn from the simple fact that fear can, and will, hold us back. In this chapter, I share my journey of recognizing and walking through fear while sifting through the emotional, behavioral, and spiritual layers that have built up throughout my life.

FEAR. WHAT EXACTLY DID FEAR LOOK LIKE FOR ME?

For many years it was a *fear of fat*. Becoming fat, being fat—and this fear led to an unhealthy relationship with food. Beyond my fear of fat, I never considered myself to be a fearful person—I'm adventurous, risk-taking, bold—I took chances in life and created opportunities. As I moved forward boldly in my career and accomplishments however, I used food as something to control; I blindly thought that by controlling food and my weight I would control the rest of life's problems. This was a distraction from dealing with deep-rooted fears and uncomfortable emotions that I carried around with me. It felt easier to pretend that fear did not exist. But fear was lurking in the shadows within the very identity of who I was. And you can't hide from your shadows. They will be there to confront you.

Reflecting on my younger years, I can recall how challenging it felt to be understood, heard, and accepted. Perhaps it was because I was half Asian living in a predominantly white community or maybe I inherited dysfunction factors that many of us take on through the generations. I concluded during my childhood that *I was not enough, I was different and that was not okay, and that I was not safe to be me.* These false beliefs would continue to affect me throughout the years and showed up in the form of an eating disorder, drug abuse, toxic relationships, and a low sense of purpose, worth, and self-esteem. It was around age eleven or twelve when my eating disorder first started. I never had issues with weight as a child, but during sixth and seventh grade I put on weight as I started to abuse food and overeat. I remember comments about my weight-gain from peers and family friends and that, paired with my already fragile sense of self, birthed my preoccupation around food, obsession with weight, and an association between my weight and my value. I had starvation fixation that led to bulimia for over twenty years.

It started as anorexia. A typical day for me (when not in school) would involve scouring the internet for weight-loss exercises and pro-anorexia sites. I would meticulously count calories and allow myself one apple, two saltine crackers, and a few bowls of Lipton's chicken noodle soup. I would add more water to the quick packets. Remember that instant soup mix? It was mostly water, no calories. I allowed myself no more than four hundred calories per day. I obsessively stood on the scale. At some point it became necessary for me to eat and so I ate—and ate and ate . . . my eating disorder then shifted into a binge- and purge-cycle, also known as bulimia. At my worst, I was vomiting over ten times per day. It consumed me in a way that gave me no time for anything else. It wasn't like I woke up and thought, *I'm going to start my eating disorder today.* It was more like, *I need to be perfect and I need to feel in control.* The obsession with weight and control, using food as a distraction, and the resultant bulimia was my attempt to bury my fears. This behavior numbed the uncomfortable sensations of what I did not want to feel.

KEEPING UP APPEARANCES: LOOKS CAN BE DECEIVING

For many years, I could not go after my dreams with confidence and trust; in fact, I did not even explore what I wanted for myself, so my dreams were made up of what I thought would make me happy, such as continuing with my business degree and curating a perfect external image of myself that appeared to "have it all together." Fear kept me stuck doing what I thought I had to do for success—it told me that I was not good enough just being me, that I must be better and I must be more. Fear lied and I listened.

I can look back now and see how I let fear get in the way. I would diminish myself repeatedly, making it easy to be mistreated and taken advantage of by others. I selected relationships and situations that created circumstances that left me feeling taken for granted and silenced. Fear was woven into my life and screaming in my ear—showing up in the form of toxic relationships, isolation, perfectionism, self-criticism, disconnection, and overall dissatisfaction. Although there was a part of me that knew that living this way was damaging, it did not register with me. It was almost separate from me. It was a void and a feeling of disconnection from who I really was—from myself and my spirit. Instead of leaning into fear and working through it, for many years I turned to alcohol, drugs, and food in an attempt to ignore it. The destructive cycle was binge, purge, shame, repeat.

I continued to work away at my degree throughout my early twenties because "it was the right thing to do." Nevermind that I was failing full semesters and also taking stimulant drugs to keep myself focused. I would do drugs and starve myself for days, drink, binge, purge, repeat—it was a recipe for disaster.

Nobody knew that I was living with an emptiness within; I did not form close relationships for fear of someone learning my secrets. I was an actress in my life; external satisfactions were the driver and I was living a double life—a lie essentially—that left me isolated, starved, and alone. It occupied so much of my time, my mind, and my life. After finally finishing my degree in human resources management, I went on to become a realtor. I was always striving for external accomplishments and being a realtor was the perfect lifestyle for someone living a double-life as a bulimic, a drinker, and who needed to escape from herself at intermittent times throughout the day. The ability to hold down a nine-five job is a challenge for someone who struggled in the ways I have mentioned. I crafted a lifestyle that allowed me to turn away and not deal with the fear, the unpleasantries of myself, and the reality that I was living out of alignment with who I was meant to be.

Changes Needed to be Made: How I Came to Recognize, Address, and Heal

I could have kept side-stepping the pain inside of myself, leaving it unrecognized, leaving it alone. Thankfully, on a deeper level, my soul was calling to me—*enough.* My first step towards healing and releasing fear was to make better choices for myself through exploration; I began to wonder, *perhaps there was a life beyond bulimia?* It was amazing how once I set my intention to heal, the journey began and the universe put everything and everybody in my path to bring me closer to my deepest healing.

My road to recovery and ability to release my fear of fat did not happen overnight, but rather, through a series of choices, steps, setbacks (or so I thought of these moments at the time), and then further commitment to myself. It was a spiritual journey and an awakening on many levels. It took time, mindfulness, money, exploration of different modalities, and following the inner-path of knowing what was right for me. I fell off the wagon. I got back on. I tapped into each layer of my personal onion; I worked through years of conditioning, false belief systems, physical and emotional traumas, and inherited dysfunctions.

My intuition told me that I had a road to take, one less traditional and clinical than what was currently advertised as practical eating disorder treatment. I tried all of it: acupuncture, body talk, heilkunst, reiki, heart math, hypnotherapy—if I felt pulled to it I tried it. My most consistent modality was heilkunst, which is a German word meaning "the art of making whole" and describes a form of homeopathic medicine. With my inventory of fears and confusions and partial delusions on the table, I was committed to unmasking my fear of fat and to understand what was behind it. Where did this examination lead? I had to open myself up to that which I most wanted to resist: a ton of emotions, beliefs, stories, and pain.

Once you start leaning into fear, it releases its grip. It took a willingness to unlearn patterns like black-and-white thinking and detach from the narratives I wanted to hold on to. I learned the power of our subconscious minds and the importance of feeding our minds with positive thoughts. I had to feel emotions—this one was big for me. By staying emotionally numb for so many years, I was trying to save myself from experiencing grief, but I was also preventing myself from experiencing true joy. I learned to feel the emotions associated with the fear and embrace them, without judgment or guilt. As I write this chapter, I am still working to discover where my body may be holding onto fear. Emotional release can get messy, but it feels so good at the same time. I had to confront areas where I did not take action, times when I procrastinated and made excuses. Inaction will keep the fear alive and allow it to breed, paralyzing our body and mind. There were many opportunities when I could have told myself that I couldn't or shouldn't; I could have made up a story about why it would be easier to keep the bulimia and not move through the fear of coping without it. But there was that part of me—the part called by my spirit—that had to continue moving forward. This happened in a very interesting way—it was more of a gradual unfolding, like following a crumb trail, rather than a straightforward and linear experience. It was small shifts that made up a larger picture over time and a combination of emotional, behavioral, and spiritual applications that carried me forward and brought me a tremendous amount of growth.

The more that I aligned with myself and removed the blockages getting in the way of who I was and what I wanted for myself, the more I released the bad patterns of behaviors.

I recognized my fear of fat for what it really was: a distraction and a temporary bandage to soothe feelings of inadequacy, unworthiness, and shame. I then understood that my fears had very little to do with food and more to do with an idea that I would always fall short of who I needed and wanted to be.

As time continued, it became easier for me to eat and I was able to consistently nourish my body without guilt, judgment, limitations, boundaries, or fear. The "I can't eat this" mentality was gone. I noticed my efforts finally resulted in me being able to naturally eat without guilt. I was not in a fight with myself over food. I never thought I could be free from my unhealthy obsession with it, but fear began to loosen its hold on me, and then, suddenly, there I was, happily going out for meals and not creating excuses to leave right after to throw up or binge. I was free to fuel my body without limitations or guilt.

THE PRESENT: COMING HOME

When I removed the eating disorder, the substance abuse, and the habit of wanting to disassociate, I was choosing to embrace life in the most authentic way and suddenly life showed up for me.

Interestingly, it was my journey through fear and discovery of self that led me to my true potential, passion, and calling—irony at its finest.

My love for self-development, transformation, inspiration, creativity, and magic guided me to start my blog, podcast, and coaching business. I can recall several points of synchronicities and auspicious signs—the powers of divine timing and magic—continuing to further strengthen my relationship with my spirit. The combination of choices that created the pathways for immense learning and undoing has led me to freedom. I do not fear any specific foods and there are no "good" or "bad" foods like there were before. I eat what I want when I am hungry, and stop when I am full. I don't think about food obsessively; I eat like a *regular* person. I know this sounds like a seemingly simple task for most, but this is an extraordinary achievement for me.

When it comes to fear, understanding it and working through it, I believe that everybody has their own unique path that they must discover for themselves. Finding strength where there was once fear holds so much power and inspiration and I recognize the power of transformation within myself and for others. I also recognize that we can utilize our biggest pains as our greatest gifts; bringing understanding to the meaning "from Karma to Dharma."

FEAR AS A TEACHER

I could say fear is a liar, but in many ways, I can thank fear for what it has shown me about myself and the universe. Fear has taught me to become aware of the parts of myself seeking comfort and trying to play it safe—the parts of myself that are scared to move forward. There are still times when I experience fear, especially as I continue to grow and develop, and this is totally okay. It can show itself in the form of feeling *stuck*, both physically and mentally, which leads to inaction. I feel stifled, paralyzed, and emotionally drained—sometimes I get angry. I am even exploring emotions stuck in body parts, like my hip. With greater awareness, instead of shying away from fear, I can lean in and explore what this means for me and what it is trying to tell me. In doing this, I become closer to what I feel my purpose is in this life. As I write this, I wonder about you, the person reading this. What are your fears and what might they be trying to teach you? Let fear's whispers tell you what it is you need to hear. Fear has kept me stuck and small, but it has also been a teacher, a mentor, and a shadow bringing greater meaning and understanding to my life. I don't look at fear as something that needs to be fully eliminated, but rather explored as it comes up during different seasons of our lives. Of course, our best teachers are not always liked, nor welcomed, in the beginning, but we thank them in the end.

I will forever be grateful for fear as a teacher.

CHAPTER SEVEN

FEAR IS A GIFT: DISCOVERING IT AT THE TOP OF THE STAIRS

"We can choose to live in the shadow of our fears, or we can bravely turn toward the light and let our strength of spirit overshadow and conquer them."

Lorene Hughes

www.scarybunnybefit.com

ig: @scarybunnybefit | fb: @ScaryBunnyBeFit
li: Lorene B Hughes | t: @ScaryBunnyBeFit

Lorene Hughes

Lorene Hughes is the fearless leader of Scary Bunny Be Fit, a fitness and wellness coaching business designed to help women bravely embrace a healthy lifestyle. She lives in Calgary, Alberta with her not-so-scary bunny, Bella.

Lorene was not always a fearless leader. Extremely shy, and team-sport-adverse, she was scarred by her high school physical education experience. She left grade school loathing sports and exercise of any kind. In her twenties she ventured into an aerobics class; she loved it, was good at it, and the classes felt comfortable and safe. She attended the program multiple times per week for more than a decade, afraid to branch out and try something new.

The journey from discovering the joy of exercise to becoming a fitness instructor and entrepreneur was a long one, fraught with self-doubt. Today, Lorene believes she has much to share with other women. Besides teaching multiple exercise programs, she has discovered first-hand the power of community in overcoming fear, and the importance of exercise as a means of living well and building confidence and self-esteem.

T he trip to my local Co-op store should have played out like any other trip. It is late Friday afternoon and I am making a quick grocery run to pick up items to get me through the weekend. Here in Calgary, Alberta it is late March and spring is a long way off for us. Temperatures are still very cold and the snow does not want to leave. Walking toward the store, my focus is divided between finding my shopping list and juggling the reusable shopping bags that I am taking in with me. And then it hit me: the hard, cold, wet ground, and the puddle that I would like to think softened the landing. Wait . . . what?!

Whether it is the cold water I am sitting in, or being mortified by what just happened, I am up like a ninja, making my way to the curb to do a quick assessment of the right hip and hand on which I landed. Soaking wet, but relieved that both my body and my mobile phone were unscathed, I walk back to the car prepared to take this as a not-so-gentle sign that this trip could wait another day.

As I look back on this incident, it strikes me that I am not as immune to falling as I thought. As a fitness instructor, I teach multiple classes per week and consider myself strong and flexible. As a highly active adult, I walk, hike, garden, and travel. Falling only happens to "old" people . . . right?

When people reach a certain age of maturity, a.k.a. "old" or "older," they begin to develop certain fears around aging, specifically, physical aging. Falling alone has the potential of contributing to all the fears associated with aging—becoming a burden, being incapable of living alone or caring for their spouse or partner, and social isolation. Second to that would be the fear of creating a bucket list—travel, theatre, gardening, walking the dog, hiking, skiing—and not having the time, energy, or mobility to complete it. What I cannot help wondering is, at what point did we develop these fears? Why are some people so paralyzed by these fears that they do not do what they want to do, and could do, because they are afraid that their bodies will betray them? What about those people who risk doing more than they should to prove that they are still capable and become injured in the process? And why do others rise so far above their fears that they leave those of us who think we are fit standing with our mouths open in awe?

Fear of Physical Aging, Then and Now: Putting it Into Perspective

My family history is one of healthy and vibrant longevity. Typically, my relatives lived out their lives in their own homes. My grandfather was still driving his car in his nineties and my great-grandfather was riding his bicycle at a similar age until someone took it away from him. They were two generations that did not have spaces dedicated to supporting even a basic level of fitness nor did they have a treadmill, bicycle, or a set of weights in their basements. They lived through scarcity yet ate well, and survived a great depression, and two world wars. If they could do it, what reason did I have to expect anything less from my parents or even myself? We have so much more at our disposal than they did: organized fitness classes; plentiful, healthy food options; and health and wellness professionals who dedicate their lives to better understanding the human body. What could we have to fear? We should easily live well into our hundreds!

What I wish I could go back and ask all my relatives is: did they have the same fears around physical aging that we have today, or are our fears a product of our twenty-first-century world? Since nursing homes did not exist until the 1960s, families took care of their elderly family members, often bringing them into their own homes to care for them as they aged. For many of us today, the decline of traditional family units means that we do not necessarily have a spouse, partner, or children to care for us in our later years. We fear that if we do not age strong enough to care for ourselves, that a stranger will be tasked to care for us, or worse yet, that we will end up in a nursing home.

PHYSICAL AGING 2.0

In the mid-1960s, my parents built a bi-level home in Calgary in which to raise their growing family. Family history had shown us that "until death do us part" applied to the family home as much as to the loving marriage contained within it, and my parents were showing no signs of changing that tradition. As empty-nesters, they could have lived anywhere, but they were content to remain in the family home. There was a very brief point in time, after we kids had left the nest, when Mom and Dad looked briefly at downsizing into a smaller home, but I expect the process of acquiring a new home, downsizing everything that they had collected over the years, and starting over with new neighbours in a new neighbourhood was just too much to take on in middle age. So, they stayed.

Over the years, Mom and Dad were active in their own way. But not the kind of active that necessarily leads to the best results when it comes to safely aging in place, particularly when that place has stairs. Three kids running around the house, up and down the stairs, kept Mom active, as did keeping the house spotless. She was an excellent cook and kept carpets vacuumed, hardwood floors polished, and furniture dusted. But she was not "outdoorsy" and was never interested in formal exercise of any kind. Dad was always active. Growing up on a farm in Northern Alberta, he was accustomed to physically-demanding work. As a professional engineer, he spent his early years working on oil rigs prior to moving into an office position. At home, he maintained the yard and had outdoor pursuits that brought him joy—hunting, fishing, horseback riding, gold-panning, and cross-country skiing. Mom and Dad enjoyed travelling, and, in their sixties, traveled to the UK, navigating England, Ireland, and Wales by car.

Married sixty-one years, they had no reason to fear that they would not enjoy their remaining years together in their own home. They expected that together, and with the help of family, they would be able to successfully deal with any issues that came their way.

FEAR-LESS: A SOLID PHYSICAL FOUNDATION, POSITIVE ATTITUDE, AND A PLAN

Oftentimes, we can do everything right, and our bodies will still betray us. This was the case with Dad. In 2015, he became eligible to receive a much-needed hip replacement. Did he have reason to fear? Absolutely . . . Dad was eighty-eight years old. But he was always a planner and he knew the risks. He believed that if he were physically ready to receive a new hip, he could mitigate the risks. He drew inspiration from his older brother, who had successfully received a new hip in his early nineties, and began to plan for his success. He attended the prescribed pre-surgery exercise classes. Post-surgery, he attended the physiotherapy appointments and continued to do the exercises at home. With an expired passport in hand, he renewed it for another ten years.

Dad had been in an enviable position where his hip replacement was concerned. Considering his age, he had started with a strong physical foundation, developed throughout his active life, and advanced it further to meet his fears head-on and successfully rise above them. His attitude remained positive and he visualized himself returning pain-free to the activities that he enjoyed, even planning a second trip to the Yukon Territories with my brother Colin.

AT THE BASE OF THE STAIRS, WHERE FEAR BECOMES A MOUNTAIN

Mom was much more cautious as she became older. She knew her limitations, asking Dad for extra help around the house, and no one displayed greater respect for stairs than she did. While she never admitted to being concerned about managing the stairs in the house, it was clear by her actions that she did not take their risk lightly. Appropriate footwear, hands holding firmly onto the handrails, and taking one careful stair at a time, she safely made her way up and down them daily—until the day when she missed the last stair and broke her hip. What followed was a two-and-a-half-month stay in hospital that left no room in Mom's life, or ours, for anything but fear. Where Dad's surgeon had no concerns with his age of eighty-eight years, when it came to a full hip replacement, the prognosis for a full and speedy recovery was not as favourable when it came to Mom's broken hip at age eighty-four. At the heart of the issue was that she had never taken part in any form of exercise other than what daily housework provided. Over the years, she had not developed sufficient strength to give her the physically solid foundation that she would require to get her up walking again. Imagine Mom's fears, and ours, when her surgeon decided that she was not physically strong enough to recover from her broken hip and must therefore move into a nursing home—cruelly adding that most people who go into a nursing home following a fall survive less than a year.

No one wakes up one day and chooses to move into a nursing home. That is one of those life choices, like death, which is not usually ours to make. Fear loomed up in front of our eyes as a collage of all the challenges that lay ahead. Mom's list of fears was long, but at the top was never being able to go home to Dad. As occupational therapists stopped coming around and the job of finding a suitable nursing home was thrust upon us, reality set in and the fears intensified for all of us. Mom's fear turned into anger toward us for not being able to save her from the fate of a nursing home, and ours into frustration with the unkind system that we were dealing with. Fear of failing Mom was agonizing.

DRIVEN BY FEAR: THE GREAT MOTIVATOR

If ever there was a time for Mom to regret her choice to not engage in formal daily exercise during her lifetime, this was it. Harnessing the fear of what Mom's future, and Dad's, looked like without help fueled my resolve to do whatever it would take to ensure that Mom's time in a nursing home was short.

She had never been open to allowing me to exercise with her in the past, but she was going to have to agree to it now if she had any hope of going home. She had to make up for years of physical inactivity in a brief period; we had our work cut out for us.

As a fitness instructor, I have a plethora of tools of the trade. While still in the hospital, I went to work helping Mom gain strength in her arms and legs using hand weights and fitness bands when seated in a chair. Dad suggested exercises that she could do while still in bed, based on his hip replacement experience. I was grateful to have Colin, my brother, there to help motivate Mom. His ability to cheer Mom on with his unique style of humor was invaluable in creating a lighter side to this challenging plan. Mom was the wildcard; there were good days when her fear of the future empowered her, and other days when it deflated her.

Climbing Back Up the Mountain

The day came for us to move Mom into the nursing home that we had carefully chosen for her. Looking around at the residents in wheelchairs, some exercising with the recreation director, others dozing where they sat, my heart broke for Mom. The staff was friendly and welcoming, but, without a miracle, this was clearly not a place that anyone walked out of. The fear was suffocating, but we kept reminding Mom that with enough work, she could go home again.

The clock was ticking. For Mom to rise above her fear of never going home again, she would have to re-climb the very mountain from which she fell . . . the stairs. It was her Mount Everest, and we were her guides. Our first task was to convince the staff that we were serious in our resolve to rehabilitate Mom and obtain permission to continue the exercises that I had started in the hospital. Nursing homes have protocols and they are created exclusively for keeping residents safe, fed, engaged, and entertained. We were asking for so much more and often met with resistance.

Reimagining Fear into Milestones

I reimagined Mom's all-encompassing fear of not going home to Dad into a series of milestones. Dad or I exercised daily with Mom and the occupational therapists at the nursing home. When Dad's health began to deteriorate, I exercised with Mom exclusively. Sadly, within the first year in the nursing home, we lost Dad to cancer. Mom's resolve to continue to exercise was unwavering, but her fear shifted from not being able to go home to Dad, to going home and taking care of herself without him.

Dad's passing had left a massive void in our lives on so many levels, but even without him, I continued to execute our plan to rehabilitate Mom. Colin soon joined me, exercising with Mom on alternate days. She enjoyed Colin being there; all the female residents and staff made such a fuss over him and it made her proud. Progress came faster and the stronger Mom became, the more motivated she was. Even though we knew in our hearts that Mom could never go home again, every physical gain we helped her to make would allow us to live some of our lives outside of the walls of the nursing home. It was the best we could do.

We bid farewell to Mom in June of 2019; our hearts broken, but also full of immeasurable pride at all that she had accomplished in two short years. Against all odds, Mom's fear of never going home had empowered her to keep moving forward. She developed the strength to transfer from her wheelchair to the bed, the toilet, and most importantly, to my car. That milestone alone brought with it the reward of attending Vertigo Theatre performances in year two. Mom learned to walk short distances with a walker, and while she never made it back to her own home, she made it to my home for Easter dinner in 2019. Mom conquered her Everest . . . she had climbed the stairs at the nursing home, so she could climb mine.

Reflecting on Fear as a Gift

Has Mom and Dad's journey given me reason to fear physical aging? No, but it has absolutely changed my perspective. Even though our family history is one of longevity, Mom and Dad's story could not present a clearer argument for the importance of staying healthy and physically strong through every age and stage of life. We deserve to enjoy every item on our bucket list, but doing so depends on us having the mobility to do so.

What I did not expect, as I relived my memories of the past four years, was to recognize that fear is a gift. As Mom and Dad each conquered their own physical challenges, what motivated and empowered them both to keep moving forward through it all was fear. Without fearing the worst, they would not have achieved their best, and their lives would have looked quite different. As challenging as their journey was for all of us, it allowed us to spend more time together, and for that gift, I am grateful.

Fear may begin as cold dread in the pit of our stomach—it can feel suffocating, and force us to take a road less traveled. But it can also bring out a strength of spirit in us that we never knew existed, and conquering it can leave our heart bursting with pride.

Fear is a gift.

CHAPTER EIGHT

FEAR OF STICKING ONE'S NECK OUT

"The mental drumbeat of 'you're not good enough' and 'you're helping wrong' does stunt privileged white women who are looking to be good allies to disadvantaged groups diverse in race, ethnicity, gender, ability, sexual orientation, and background."

Rebecca Juetten

www.littlecrabpress.ca

fb: @LittleCrabEdu

Rebecca Juetten

Rebecca Juetten (also known in Chinese as Zhū Tíng - 朱婷) got her BA in Pacific and Asian studies, China concentration, from the University of Victoria in 2004. She has been a student of Mandarin Chinese since 1998, as well as a certified English as a foreign language (ESL/EFL) teacher for over fifteen years (CELTA certified since 2011). In 2015, she created Little Crab Educational Press, a company that develops and produces children's bilingual edutainment products, specializing in English and Mandarin based materials. Rebecca's lifelong interest in writing came to the forefront after the birth of her son in 2017, leading to her first-ever long-form writing project. Rebecca lives with her family in beautiful Victoria, British Columbia, Canada.

When I think about fears and my life, for the most part, I am proud of myself. Maybe it's because of my privilege, or maybe I actually deserve to call myself brave for things I've done. When I was young, bravery was setting my sights on auditioning and subsequently being chosen for roles I wanted in small stage productions. Later, it was flying to a foreign country alone, which I did on more than one occasion, often staying for months at a time in a place where English is not the official language. And, it was conceiving of, writing, and self-publishing a bilingual kids book and having to (*gulp*) do self-marketing; getting pregnant and delivering a baby; and being a mother. Maybe it's both privilege and bravery mixed together. At any rate, if I felt fear at those times, it didn't stop me.

Here's one jigsaw piece of what it was like to be this socially-minded, white, middle-class, straight, Canadian cis-girl growing up in the 1980s in British Columbia: Raised by two of the hardest working teachers I've ever witnessed (one elementary, one high school), both absolute pros, I was exposed to things like having CBC Radio News on during dinner and getting my questions about local and world affairs answered by my parents in real-time. I was drawn to the idea of politics as a space where people could gather, make a collective statement of values, and struggle to make the world better as a team, as a group. Before I knew "intersectional" was a word, I intrinsically knew that any such group I might become part of would have to be intersectional for it to work. It was just a given.

Of course, the glow of an altogether happy childhood continued to make way for the *real world*. One example being, as a child I wanted to know much more about local First Nations peoples and never understood why their clear-even-to-a-grade-schooler, since-time-immemorial presence in Canada wasn't a central theme of public school social studies, at the *very* least. (If my schools had offered Lekwungen as a second language, it's highly likely I would have taken it. *But, whom could I have asked? I couldn't simply flip through the ol' white pages!*). As I grew up, it gradually became clearer why certain knowledge wasn't available or easily accessible to me, or to other kids like me. I developed a deeper awareness of all the evils human beings are capable of, and this further confirmed my feelings about how ridiculous anti-minority sentiments are and why they should be countered by people in positions of privilege. When people refuse to support efforts toward any kind of reconciliation (not just Canada's big-R reconciliation process between settlers and First Nations, but for any issues between the beneficiaries of the patriarchy and everyone else) they often justify their positions by saying things like, "those sins were not *caused by* people of the present." That kind of willful ignorance of other people's humanity is exasperating to me.

Part of what I think makes you a good person is to find a way you can stick your neck out for people who are less advantaged than you—to represent those who (so far) can't get their voice heard on their own. Listen, join others who are doing good, and use your strength for the better. The main problem is, I think, somewhere between childhood and adulthood what seemed to count as "doing good" became a grayer area, and the "join others" part feels harder now. While I try to avoid being utterly insufferable, and to know my audience on my social media channels, and to shine my light on the positive and not just the perpetually negative, I'm sure that publicly expressing my values or political opinions makes some people who already know me want to roll their eyes. I am also not particularly afraid of insults from strangers for merely engaging in social issues in some form of public arena. Any insult directed toward a woman that I have heard or read has been and will be said to any woman, for any reason, at any time. In that way, it's easier to be the recipient of *some* of the grossest behavior that gets spewed at women: understanding that this vitriol is ubiquitous and often anonymous can help to take away the emotional stab it's intended to produce in you personally. I think what I fear is not negative feedback coming from strangers online, nor from friends and acquaintances so much, but rather it's the potential of hearing it from the actual disadvantaged people whose cause I might want to join. If they tell me essentially, "You aren't helping right" and I take them at their word (which you should do if you say you respect others), then why would I continue "helping" now that I know I am causing harm? While intention is seldom any excuse for actual (negative) results, I used to think intention would be *weighed with* the actual results, as opposed to the results alone bearing all the weight. But that assumption was disproved in the very time and place that I would have otherwise expected any political or citizen seeds of activism in me to flourish: the women's center of my alma mater, 2005. Over the previous six years, this was the place where I had developed my understanding of what other straight, white, body-positive, anti-racist, anti-ableist, cis-female allies looked and sounded like. It's also the place where my confidence to fight for what I believe in politically went into a kind of stasis.

One day, I was called into a meeting with the director of the center, a white woman named Jen. She informed me that she had received complaints about me from "some of" the women who use the center. I recall often being involved in spontaneous group conversations of maybe four to twenty people that lasted anywhere from ten minutes to what must have been much longer, as we all killed time between classes. We purposefully discussed controversial things, issues the women's center was advocating for, and all the stuff you would expect to hear at any women's center at practically any university in the world.

My recollection of the complaints against me was as follows:

1) *You are "too loud":* It was unclear if this was meant strictly in terms of volume; in the center, there could, at times, be multiple conversations happening all at once. Sure, I'm often louder than a lot of people, but I am also not a provokingly, unrelentingly loud person. So, it could have been meant in terms of the general enthusiastic energy I often have when I speak.

2) *You take up too much "space"*: Seriously? My physical body? I am six feet tall and for most of my adult life, close to or over two-hundred pounds. Bit of a head-scratcher, that one, coming from supposed champions of body positivity, right? So if they didn't mean my actual body, my . . . personality, then? Was I supposed to know ahead of time to change my personality in order to avoid this criticism?

And:

3) To quote Jen: *"Some of the women here feel that you have said things which are homophobic, fat-phobic, and racist."* According to her, I made them feel *". . . unsafe in this space."*

A flood of thoughts scrambled my brain and that sickly, prickly rush of embarrassment filled my body. I scoured my memory for stories I had recounted at the center the past several months, trying to guess which ones could have been offensive, and in which way(s).

Was it that time I had come in from a crowded bus ride and told some people in the center about an incident right after it had happened? In that particular story, I had taken a cramped bus ride to campus and standing shoulder-to-shoulder with me had been a young Asian guy and a young white woman. The woman had decided to strike up a conversation with me, and to my shock and deep discomfort, had pivoted partway through to saying incredibly ignorant and racist things about Asian people, seemingly unaware of the guy standing between us (if he was paying attention to our conversation, he didn't show it). With a tone of incredulity, I recounted how I had tried to push back against this woman's opinions because they had offended me, and I couldn't stomach being a silent bystander—*literally standing idly by* during a racist rant. When telling the story, I pointed out the irony in that woman thinking I would agree with her because I was another white person. She wouldn't have known I had been lovingly studying Mandarin Chinese and Chinese culture since I was fifteen. You can't assume anything about anyone just because they share your skin tone.

I do loathe when people who claim to be non-racist hide behind expressions like "I'm just quoting someone else" without even so much as reading the room. But, while I had probably direct-quoted some of the things the racist lady said, which had offended me, I would have done so *because I trusted* the women there to consider me to be *anti*-discrimination. If using quotes was what had offended them, I would have done so strictly to contrast my *actual* opinions and offer context as to how offensive the scenario had been to me. Wasn't I in a "safe space" with "like-minded" women who would understand where I was coming from because we had already been engaging in conversations about homophobia, fat-phobia, and racism over a significant period of time? I thought they were there for one of the same reasons I was: to feel better-equipped at grappling with controversial topics like race, gender, sexual orientation, and so on, which tend to bleed into politics. Provocative conversations lead to political will, and having political will is the only way to affect positive changes in how the government deals with our rights.

At this point in the meeting, I felt shunned. I was sitting on some weirdly low couch and Jen was perched on her office chair above me. I remember being frustrated that I felt so small as she was telling me I was too big. I wanted to respond by showing respect for these mystery women who were my accusers because, for all I knew, I *had* stepped on a proverbial rake when around them, and their feelings, though completely anonymous, mattered to me. But, after listening to Jen and eventually sputtering to respond, I was horrified to discover I had zero composure and even fewer tissues. I found myself ugly-crying through an attempt to express how deeply sad I was that anyone could have felt that I, of all people, was an *actual threat* to them. Jen remained stone-faced, occasionally appearing bored. She listlessly looked around for something I could use to sop up my face. I believe someone was sent to grab me some scratchy toilet paper at one point. Eventually, I left her office and later left a response letter at the center. I doubt it was ever read. Here are some excerpts:

109

Jen said that it is "not the responsibility of a woman of color to tell a woman of privilege what it is like to be a woman of color" . . . *Despite the fact that I already agree with that point* [insert: I have never in my life asked a woman of color, "Gee, what's it like to be (your race)?"], *I feel the reason that I was given as to why I will not be receiving help to understand how I hurt these women is inappropriate. Jen informed me that if I wanted to learn more about racism, homophobia, fat-phobia, etc, then I was "welcome to use the library." Certainly the library is a great place to learn about those issues, but, I can guarantee that I will not find the solution to the problem any individual woman has with me personally in any book. To read any of the books in the center and assume that they accurately portray the personal history, or personal sense of boundaries of any one woman in the center would be totally false. I take responsibility for how I react to something, and if someone has hurt me, I am not going to rely on a book to explain to that person how to fix things.*

. . . Also, to imply that because I identify as white, straight, and from a middle-class household it naturally follows that I am racist, homophobic, and fat-phobic, then that is prejudice. And I might add, if my "presence," or how much "space" I take up is part of why these women are afraid to speak to me, then that is discrimination, too. Physically, I cannot shrink, and non-physically I can't stop being myself. Don't confuse (being) confident with confrontational, or strength with aggression. And remember, things are not always as they seem. Maybe I'm much less confident than you think I am. Maybe I am much more approachable than you think I am.

. . . If you didn't know it before just from talking to me, then let me make something perfectly clear: I abhor racism, homophobia, and fat-phobia, but I also recognize that that doesn't necessarily mean my soul is completely clean of them. Whatever I find of them, I want to purge.

Someone with my support system, my anti-prejudice values, lack of fear of public speaking, personal interest in history and politics, level of education, and all my other privileges, should feel no barrier to social activism or entering the professional political realm; in fact, she should be *empowered toward* it, especially when people are always saying, "Don't worry about what other people think" and "Just be yourself." But what if the cause you are drawn to is *all about* what other people think because *it's about other people,* not you? You have to consider that those in whichever cause you may be inclined to join will in some way make a judgment about whether you qualify to be on the team. Thus, the mental drumbeat of "you're not good enough" and "you're helping wrong" does stunt privileged white women looking to be good allies to disadvantaged groups diverse in race, ethnicity, gender, ability, sexual orientation, and background.

Over the years, I've sought ways to not just be, as Henry Rollins calls it, a "keyboard activist," raising awareness online of things she finds to be unjust whilst, in actuality, merely broadcasting a hollow kind of performative empathy for show. So, among other actions, I sign and share petitions, I donate money when I can, I make signs and go to protests, I vote and I promote voting. And I know it would be pathetic and ironic to complain about my experience—according to Merriam-Webster online, my first name has *literally* become a pejorative term: *Becky* is increasingly functioning as an epithet, and being used especially to refer to a white woman who is ignorant of both her privilege and her prejudice.[1] My women's center experience didn't make me spitefully renounce all feminist causes—I don't do "bitter" very well—but, it did make me want to be a public participant of them less often and left me wondering how anyone, especially women, ever progress into politics. In this arena, it's especially unclear where and when we are supposed to insert ourselves versus wait to be invited in. However, I did face fears writing about this topic with honesty, and I will continue striving to live with integrity, to have conversations that break the ice with others politically, and to represent a *different* kind of Becky (with the good ~~hair~~ heart).

---

1   "Words We're Watching: 'Becky,'" Merriam-Webster, accessed August 2020, https://www.merriam-webster.com/words-at-play/words-were-watching-becky.

CHAPTER NINE

FEARING LESS: FINDING COURAGE AS WE AGE

"The more you do, the less you fear."

Sharon Hughes-Geekie

jumpstartcomm.ca

fb: @sharon.hughesgeekie
li: Sharon Hughes-Geekie | t: @JumpstartAnd

Sharon Hughes-Geekie

Sharon Hughes-Geekie is a writer, speaker, and entrepreneur. She is the owner of JumpStart Communications and Business Development, and more recently, From the Bear's Chair. Mother of two adult children, she lives with her giant dog Winston in Kelowna, British Columbia.

Sharon believes fear is often self-doubt in disguise. Fear, in its truest form, keeps us safe. Self-doubt prevents us from taking risks, seizing opportunities, and enjoying everything life has to offer, particularly as we age. Drawing upon personal insights, and experience gained over more than a decade as a director with a national home health care company, Sharon provides tips and truths to help us live bravely at any age.

Sharon holds a Bachelor of Arts in Creative Writing from the University of Victoria.

The older we get, the more fearful we become. As a child, I was considered reckless. I grew up in a family that was cautious, conservative, and risk-averse. The proverbial "black sheep" of my clan, I was constantly pushing boundaries and doing things considered risky or "unsafe." One Saturday when I was six, my dad promised that tomorrow we would visit the zoo. Sunday arrived, dark and cloudy, canceling our day of fun. I donned my favorite jacket and bravely announced that everyone could sit around waiting for the rain; I was going to the zoo by myself. Dad said I would need something to feed the bears and handed me a tin of stewed tomatoes. Off I went—no money, no directions, no can opener. I made it three blocks before Dad drove by and picked me up.

In my teens, I discovered social activism. It started with letter writing but the more I learned the more incensed I became. The world was a mess: pollution, deforestation, the killing of innocent animals for fur. I was passionate and unfiltered—a regular placard-carrying protester. My quest for social change was hampered by my need to buy groceries and pay rent. On weekends I was a crusader but by day I worked an entry-level position for a large oil company. On the elevator to work one day, I brazenly told the oil company's top executive secretary that her full-length mink coat would look better on its original owners. Although I did not get fired, I did receive a stiff reprimand and landed an opportunity to meet her boss, the company president.

Being brave is easy when you do not fully comprehend the potential outcomes of your actions. The more you know, the more you fear.

The Terrifying Thirties

I officially became a grown-up in my thirties. My husband and I bought our first house, acquired a dog and, not long after, had our first child. All the responsibility terrified me. I was afraid of losing my job and not being able to pay the mortgage. I was afraid of being a bad parent and ruining my daughter's life, or worse, dying in a catastrophic accident and leaving her without a mother. I was afraid of the car breaking down, the house catching fire, and of losing our precocious Jack Russell, who had become a masterful escape artist.

At age thirty-six, my marriage of fourteen years ended a mere month before the arrival of our second child. I knew I would be raising two children on my own and the fear was overwhelming. Besides the obvious financial challenges, how was I going to juggle a full-time management position with a toddler and a new baby? I returned to work after a four-month maternity leave. My daughter Aly was in kindergarten, and after school care; my son Davis was in a daycare near my office, enabling me to breastfeed on my lunch break. Despite those conveniences, there was not enough of me to go around. Lonely, exhausted, overwhelmed, and struggling with depression, I discovered that hardship fosters resilience and desperation gives you the courage to ask for help.

By daring to show vulnerability and opening myself up to the assistance and support of others, I created a better life for my children.

Learning to Drive a Marshmallow

My children were raised in a close-knit rural community. Even though I was no longer part of a couple, neighbors always included us in group events with other families. My children were four and seven when we experienced our first neighborhood camping trip. I purchased a two-room tent at a garage sale and invited Deb, a single mom with children the same ages as my own, to bunk with us. Setting-up a two-room tent without any directions was beyond frustrating. We had tried just about every tent pole combination possible when a kindly dad came to our rescue and finished the job for us. That night, Deb and I awoke to noises outside the tent. A light was being shone around our campsite. We looked at each other, wide-eyed and silent. Was it a burglar? What if they tried to come into our tent? The noise subsided and the light disappeared. I quietly unzipped the tent and peered out. No one in sight. Slipping on our shoes, Deb and I ventured outside to see if anything was missing. A man was sitting outside a luxury trailer nearby. We asked him if he had seen anyone roaming around our site. He confessed it was him. His cat had disappeared and he was searching for her. Relieved, we wished him luck and returned to bed. Minutes later, rain pattered on the roof. As it grew louder, the zipper of the partition opened and four children crammed themselves into our sleeping bags. The body heat was welcome as water permeated our nylon shelter and trickled onto our beds. We cuddled and shivered until the first light of day when we piled our muddy, wet gear into our vehicles, and headed for home. I sold the tent at my next garage sale and the following year purchased a used twenty-six-foot motorhome, complete with impermeable roof, indoor plumbing, and a door that locked.

Purchasing a recreational vehicle was not an easy feat. Not only did I know nothing about RVs, I had never driven anything larger than a van. I found a thirty-year-old class C motorhome for a good price. A friend test drove it for me and delivered it to my home. The annual end-of-school camping trip was just two weeks away and I was terrified to drive my new purchase. I asked my neighbor, Blair, for a driving lesson. He calmly talked me through backing out of the driveway and turning onto the street. My heart was pounding as we rattled onto the main road, branches slashing at the windows. Blair taught me how to center the vehicle using my mirrors and when to start slowing down for a traffic light. He said I needed to relax and bounce with the vehicle—to picture myself driving a giant marshmallow. The imagery worked. As I focused on bouncing, my heart slowed, and my grip on the steering wheel loosened. Blair insisted I pull over at a child's lemonade stand. He jumped out and brought back two paper cups of lemonade. He said it was important to learn how to drive while holding a beverage so I could drink coffee on the road. There was no cup holder. I was now maneuvering an enormous marshmallow one-handed while balancing lemonade without a lid in the other. By the time I pulled back into my driveway, I was feeling much more self-assured, albeit a tad wet.

The day of the camping trip arrived. I piled the kids and the dog into the Marshmallow and took my place at the wheel— without a coffee cup. I had been "bouncing" for an hour (it felt much longer) when I happened upon a gas station I felt confident I could pull into without hitting anything. While the gas tank filled, I massaged my cramped fingers. Another thirty minutes to go. When we drove through the gate of the campground, neighbors cheered. I found our pull-through campsite, switched off the ignition, closed my eyes, and inhaled. I'd done it. I had gotten us safely to our destination. I opened my eyes. The Marshmallow was surrounded by neighborhood dads. They showed me how to put blocks behind the tires, level the vehicle, and hook up water, electricity, and septic. We were all set, and it was one of the most enjoyable camping trips we ever took.

The kids were in their teens, and the Marshmallow had developed a leaky roof (from crashing into an outhouse), when I finally gave it away. I never overcame my fear of driving "the big M." Every strong wind would cause a heart-stopping rush of adrenalin as I pictured the Marshmallow tipping over and cascading down an embankment. So why did I continue to drive it for so many years?

Summoning courage is easier when people are depending on you to be brave and supporting you to succeed.

New Experiences Build Courage

As director for a national health care company, I regularly made presentations to seniors about home safety and the importance of nutrition and exercise to quality of life. At the end of one such presentation, a spry, well-dressed gentleman approached me and asked why I bother. "Excuse me," I responded in surprise.

"People over eighty," he explained, "typically eat, sleep, and watch television. Their lives are punctuated with medical appointments or visits from family, but that's about it. If you don't try new things, you're not living—you're marking time until you die."

Before I could respond, he asked how many new things I had tried that year. I guessed three or four. "My challenge to you," he said, "is to do twelve things you have never done before. Next year, do twelve more. Do twelve new things every year until you can't. That's my advice." And with that, he walked away.

I accepted his challenge, and it changed my life. I started saying "yes" to opportunities simply because I was determined to reach my annual goal. The first year, I did things that truly terrified me. Under the guidance of an entomologist, I held a tarantula. The secret is to think of the furry little creature as a rodent and not an arachnid. I climbed up and down the steep, tiny steps of a pyramid in Mexico. I learned to snorkel, studied Spanish, painted my first picture, built a website, and trained to perform a choreographed dance routine in front of a live audience at a gala fundraiser.

The following year, my son Davis and I went to San Diego for spring break. Now in his teens, we agreed that for a new experience we would go sea kayaking. We booked a tour, hopped on a bus to La Jolla, but mistakenly got off at the wrong stop. There was a drugstore nearby and I went to ask for directions. When I came out, I told Davis we had a ride to the beach.

"You ran into someone you know in the drugstore?" he asked, incredulously.

"No," I said. "An older couple offered us a ride."

He looked alarmed: "We're getting into a car with complete strangers!"

"They seem very nice," I said reassuringly. It was obvious his stranger-danger upbringing was kicking in. His hand was firmly on the door handle the entire ride. We arrived at the place where our sea kayaking adventure was to begin and it was definitely not what I had envisioned. The waves were huge! People were surfing! Now I was fearful and it was Davis' turn to reassure.

We chose a tandem kayak so we could be together. The tour we signed up for included paddling through caves but our guide advised that the water was much too choppy and we would be forgoing that part of the expedition. I was ready to forgo the entire experience! The guide showed us how to get back into the boat if it capsized and instructed us to hit the waves head-on. I am not a good swimmer and was terrified of drowning. Davis, as it turned out, had fears of his own. He had seen a documentary about seals and sea lions attacking people, and both were swimming in close proximity to our boat. He was afraid of being pulled in and eaten.

We made it through almost the entire tour without mishap. As we approached the shore, Davis steered the kayak into a large wave, and we flipped. The boat hit me hard in the mouth as I fell into the ocean. I felt certain I had chipped my front tooth. Overcome with pain and panic, I was frantically flailing when I heard Davis calling to me, "Mom . . . stand up." I stopped struggling and uncurled my legs. I was standing. The water was waist-deep, my front tooth was fine, and the people laughing at me from the shore, I would never see again.

Experiences need not be potentially dangerous to invoke fear-like symptoms. Anything new or unfamiliar inherently causes stress, anxiety, and self-doubt, even if the experience is meant to be pleasurable. When my daughter, Aly, turned twenty-five, we celebrated by spending a night at a lavish wellness resort. Simply put, I am not a spa kind of gal. Doing nothing is a challenge for me and, if I am sitting still, my brain is in overdrive; planning the next project or making mental lists of things I need to do. This trip was clearly out of my comfort zone. Our room at the resort was opulent beyond anything we had ever experienced. We donned the white terry robes and slippers provided and headed to the spa. I took my cues from Aly who loves being pampered but was no stranger to my restlessness. Fortunately, there was lots to do. After languishing in seven aromatherapy steams and saunas, we laid our hot bodies against a wall of ice. We tried the circulation-improving Kniep hydrotherapy, walking through a knee-deep linear pool that alternates between warm and ice water. We drank herbal tea in a room where talking was prohibited; watched big flakes of snowfall as we lazed in an outdoor heated pool; ate the most amazing pistachio crème brûlée; and then retired to our Swarovski-crystal-adorned room to try out the big, comfy beds. Aly is a sound sleeper and fell asleep almost immediately. Searching for the light switch to turn off the crystals, I mistakenly turned on every light in our suite. Aly did not stir. At three a.m. I awoke to high-pitched beeping, indicating the battery on the smoke detector needed changing. Aly did not stir. I turned on the light and stood on a chair but could not reach the alarm. I called the front desk but was told there was a bad snowstorm and the night maintenance man was stuck en route. The woman on the phone promised it would be fixed as soon as they were able. I put pillows over my head to reduce the sound of the relentless warning and worried about our impending drive home in a storm. Five hours later, Aly, looking annoyingly refreshed, emerged from her bed asking, "Oh my god, what is that annoying noise?" Hastily throwing on clothes, we headed downstairs to an elaborate buffet breakfast. By the time we returned to our room, the annoying noise had stopped and the storm was subsiding.

A new or unfamiliar situation can be uncomfortable and cause apprehension. Sharing it with someone makes those feelings more manageable and the experience more enjoyable.

I Have Learned . . .

That dapper senior at my presentation changed my life. Since accepting his challenge four years ago, I have attempted more than sixty new things. These experiences have enriched my life, enhanced my relationships, and made me fear less— but there is something else. I track the new things I have done in a journal, which I review annually. Since I embarked on this journey, both my parents have died, my dog of fourteen years had to be put down, and I have lost five other close friends and relatives to a variety of diseases and ailments. When I look at the list of experiences for those years, I reflect with gratitude on the special moments I have shared with family, friends, and pets. I marvel at my accomplishments, the crazy things I have done, and despite the sadness and loss, I can honestly report that I have not had a bad year.

As we age, we become more vulnerable and legitimately have more to fear: getting sick, losing our minds, burdening our families, running out of money, breaking a hip, losing our independence. Living our best life at any age involves continually assessing risk versus reward, finding a healthy balance, and pushing ourselves to do things that make us uncomfortable. I have learned that:

- Trying new things increases confidence, improves your quality of life, and makes you a more interesting person;
- New experiences are less scary and more memorable when shared with others;
- Thinking about the people who are counting on you or cheering from the sidelines will make you brave;
- And finally, bears love stewed tomatoes!

CHAPTER TEN

HELLO, FEAR, IT'S ME AGAIN!

"Acknowledge your fear then step right through it."

Lisa Poznikoff

ig: @lisapoznikoff | fb: @lpoznikoff | li: Lisa Poznikoff
Goodreads: Lisa Poznikoff

Lisa Poznikoff

Lisa Poznikoff has lived in the West Kootenay region of British Columbia virtually all her life. The eldest of four in a close-knit family, she is ten years older than her youngest sibling. When she started her own family, Lisa took on the role of domestic engineer as though it were a job and raised two independent, strong, and talented daughters. Once her girls were old enough for her to go back to work outside the family home, Lisa found her way into many different jobs, each offering her the opportunity to learn multiple skill sets.

The adjustments and events in her life walked her to, and through, a lifetime of changes, learning opportunities, and yes, fear. Several years ago her mother suggested that Lisa write a book about her life and she jumped at this opportunity. If you ask her, she'll tell you that this project is one that has her riding a wave of fear, but she's excited to share her story of stepping through it.

Visualize acres of onion fields in springtime with long, hilled, and seeded rows. A little three-room house sits on the edge of those acres and the toddler of the house is on an adventure of a lifetime. That toddler was me in my bright red jacket, and my mom tells me that when she realized I had left her side, all she could see of me was a red dot as I walked over those hills of onions with the family dog following me. I have no memory of that adventure, but obviously I had not yet met fear. After that fearless adventure, my sister and I, being only fifteen months apart in age, became inseparable best friends and I never went anywhere alone again until I was an adult.

My childhood was good and I cannot say with certainty when it was that I first met fear. We lived in what was then the farming community of Rutland in the interior of British Columbia. Our home was somewhat isolated in those early years, so for the first five years of my life I did not have much interaction with people. Dad was a drywall contractor who often worked away from home, sometimes for weeks at a time. Mom says I would cry for days when he'd have to leave for his next job, so he would slip away without saying goodbye. The first distinct memory I do have of fear was when I went to my first day of kindergarten in the basement of a nearby church. I was afraid of all the people, kids and adults alike, and I would not let Mom out of my sight. Since my birthday falls in December, I was the youngest of my first-grade class, and because I was incredibly shy it was suggested to my parents that I be held back—maybe I'd outgrow my shyness in another year. Given the chance, once I warmed up to people, I was not shy and would become quite bubbly; to this day I am simply a quiet person and take my time getting to know others.

At an early age, I experienced an epiphany but didn't realize it for what it was until years later. My mom had a beautiful broach with a light blue stone cut in a marquise style and set as the body of a beetle. When playing with her jewelry box, I put this particular broach on the floor and began squealing, "A bug! A bug!" and jumped, bouncing safely onto the bed. After a while, I noticed that my heart had begun to race with anxiety: I was short of breath and felt afraid of that piece of jewelry even though I knew it was not a real bug. I stopped, took a breath, hesitantly picked up the broach, and carefully put it back into the jewelry box. Never did I play that game again. The feeling of fear was very unpleasant.

When I was about twelve years of age, my parents decided to pack up and move the family to the West Kootenay region of BC. Both sets of grandparents lived there, so we had visited often, but other than one friend whom I'd played with during summer visits, I didn't know anybody. Although terrified of my first day at a new school, somehow I found the strength within to overcome my fear and make more friends than I had left behind in Rutland. Just as I turned sixteen, Mom signed up my sister and me to a youth choir. Once again, I was afraid to engage with a new group of people and did not want to join. However, this time I had made a conscious decision to put fear aside and try to have fun, even accepting the offer to emcee for many of our choir performances whenever we took the stage at home and in different cities. Already shy among people, it was mind-boggling to stand alone at the microphone to speak in front of an audience, and many times I was certain my knees were audibly knocking. I once made a comment to that effect and was met with compliments on how well I had done. These supportive words helped me realize that my fear was unfounded—now I had to convince my mind of that because it always wanted to default to fear. It was then that I began to be more conscious of facing my fears and walking right through them. This was not easy, nor did it make me any less fearful, but I've learned that most of my fears are merely conjured up in my head. That beautiful broach came to mind once again.

We are born with some natural fears that are meant to be a survival mechanism, but in trying to protect us, they can also lie to us sometimes. I learned to acknowledge my fears and step right through them, which allowed me to look back and see that I'm actually okay, and having done that repeatedly has helped me to not give in to fake fears today. I am not completely without fear, but I know how to handle it now.

I met my husband during my first year of graphic design studies. We married and had two beautiful daughters, and rather than continuing with my career goal, I opted to be a stay-at-home mom. Raising our daughters brought me great joy and when I wasn't cooking, cleaning, or gardening, I was involved as a volunteer in their extracurricular activities. This often put me in the position of speaking to groups of people, something I had already learned to push through by taking deep breaths. Still, my imagination would grip me in fear and I'd become exhausted by those interactions. I realized I needed time to de-stress so that I would be able to return to social settings again. I turned to my solitary crafts—sewing, cross-stitch, embroidery—for the alone time needed to give my active mind a rest.

The opportunity to work part-time from home for a small non-profit publication presented itself and I eagerly took it on. It allowed me to finally utilize my graphic design skills, as well as the opportunity to learn a new set of computer skills. It was also an important part of my Doukhobor heritage, which I am passionate about. This part-time job of three years led to me becoming the full-time editor of that publication and a brand new fear arose. I had only been editing a small section; I did not believe that I had it in me to be an editor of the entire publication. Although I was afraid of failing the readership, I faced it head-on, just as I had learned to do from my experiences. I stepped through the fear and I flourished, becoming the youngest female editor in its sixty-year history. While I held that position over the next seven years, I enjoyed learning about publishing a periodical, as well as more about my own heritage. It is amazing what one can accomplish when fear is acknowledged, but put aside for personal growth.

Over the twenty years that we were married, there were many memorable good times with my husband, but overall we were not happy and finally agreed to go our separate ways. I would have left years sooner, but fear kept me in my comfort zone. Fear questioned me: *Do you really think you can support yourself? How will you do it alone? How will you be able to be there for your girls?* Knowing my situation, a friend asked if I might consider house-sitting for her while she was out of the country for several weeks. I agreed to it and found incredible healing by spending time with just my thoughts. That was the beginning of a major shift within me and my decisive stand against fear. My friend's partner had purchased a shop on a piece of property, which included a small home that my friend offered to rent to me. Fear tried to get a grip on me—my head dizzy, my throat constricted, my speech vanished, my heart wanting to leave my chest, and my whole body beginning to freeze. However, I accepted the offer and proceeded to take up the single life. It was not as difficult a transition as fear had me believe, and, after careful budgeting to ensure I could afford my new life, I realized that fear was wrong again and that I could make it on my own. I adjusted to my new life and was enjoying it immensely. This would only be the first step towards the further change that lay ahead.

As much as I loved my job, it was not without ongoing challenges that are a part of employment in the non-profit sector. Summer tends to be slower for the organization, so there was not a lot for me to put to print. Another friend of mine had recently moved with her husband to Saskatchewan and repeatedly invited me to visit, so I decided to accept her invitation and scheduled my trip to coincide with an annual event at the National Doukhobor Heritage Village in Veregin, Saskatchewan. Through my network, as a result of my job, I was able to arrange billeting with distant relatives, friends, and acquaintances during my entire two-week trip, but home base would be with my friend and her husband. So began the most personally liberating road trip I'd experienced complete-ly on my own since the adventure I went on beyond my fami-ly's property when I was a toddler. Every time fear questioned me I'd find a way to address it: *How will you know where to go?* I purchased a GPS, as well as road maps in case the GPS failed. *What if you have car troubles?* I took my car in for a pre-travel servicing and made sure it was in tip-top shape. I also made sure I had my cell phone and a charging cord that plugged into the car's lighter. *What if . . .* covered!

Fear has its place. It keeps us safe. However, as it sits in our heads, we should make sure that fear does not get into the driver's seat; otherwise, it will likely steer us in the wrong direction.

For this trip, I put fear into the navigator's seat to ensure a safe journey. Approaching Medicine Hat, Alberta, I decided to stop at the information center to acquire a map of Saskatchewan for my collection. Road construction in progress steered me in another direction. Departing from the pre-planned route, the GPS began voicing her instructions to get me back on track. As fear sat up at attention, I acknowledged it and thought, *let's see how the GPS will get us out of this!* I swear that if fear was a real person, I saw it begin to relax in the passenger seat and quietly enjoy the trip.

Originally, as I began planning the trip, I had put in a request that a portion of it be covered as work-related since I would be visiting brethren at a noteworthy historical site and because I planned to include an article in a future issue of the publication. My request was denied, so I made that trip a complete vacation away from any work responsibilities. However, that outcome gave me cause for thought during my long solo drive. My job came with challenges when I started, as the organization was undergoing some transition. By accepting the position, I forced the office to relocate from the neighboring city over an hour away from my hometown so that I did not have to commute over a mountain pass. Despite the support and encouragement of many, and the fact that I loved the job and enjoyed the huge learning curve, the load of multiple responsibilities that came as a result of working for a non-profit organization had begun to weigh on me. I had been considering my options two years prior, but as before, fear stepped in and kept me in my "uncomfortable comfort zone." Soon after returning from my solo trip and getting back to reality, I submitted my resignation.

It was exceptionally difficult to leave the job—I had only recently left my marriage and the job was my security. But that security came at the cost of my well-being. As frightening as it was, I essentially outstretched my arms with palms to the sky and said to the Universe, "I'm ready for something new." At the time I had no back-up plan; I broke down into tears, had my moment, and then took a deep breath and moved forward purely on my intuition, faith, and courage. Fear was not going to steer me, but was given the responsibility of navigation once again, and just as during my vacation, I found my way and everything fell into place. Feeling the need to be doing something productive with my spare time while looking for my next job, I accepted the invitation to join the board of directors of the Doukhobor Discovery Centre in Castlegar, B.C. Little did I know that a domino effect was already in motion that would result in my standing in for the museum administrator and curator position, but I had to step down from the board to successfully apply for the position. Fear reared up reminding me that, while I had the historical knowledge, I had no training for the position and I felt like I was setting myself up for failure by accepting the job.

The museum was going through some turmoil, but I was up for a new challenge. Thus, I thought, *Hello Fear. It's me again!* I acknowledged it, walked through it, and made another major change in my life. It was a brand-new learning curve, but what I discovered was that I thrive when challenges are put in front of me. With the support from my board of directors, we persevered and prevented the permanent shut down of the museum, putting it on the path to success. However, the ensuing six years of dedication took a toll on my well-being once again, and I was headed for a total burn out. I had to put my health first and resigned from my position, but in an unexpected twist of fate, my brother and his business partner had parted ways, putting his business into transition. The timing couldn't have been better. *Hey, Fear! Hello! Guess who?!* To help him get his business back on track I took the position as office manager at a temporary (but significant) pay-cut from what I'd been accustomed to. Another learning curve for me to master was bookkeeping—a much-needed skill in the local workforce. Now, I have a skill I can take anywhere with me. How long will I stay on? Who knows? For the interim, it works for me and my fear.

Yes, fear lies to us in an effort to protect us from the unknown. Where does my fear come from? Perhaps my dad going away to work for long periods of time when I was very young stirred feelings of abandonment? I am definitely an introvert and empathic but was I born that way, or did I learn to be that way as I grew up? Certainly, there are questions to ponder. I have learned that if we don't put fear aside, take chances, and step out of our comfort zone, fear will keep us trapped. It's a wonderful world of personal growth outside the comfort zone that fear keeps us in. In retrospect, I have been successfully navigating my way through it and will continue into the future. I have accepted that fear will always be my sidekick and am actually grateful for it. Signing up to write this chapter has evoked both fear and excitement in me, but I know that if I gave into fear and didn't grab this opportunity, I'd regret it. Thank you, fear, I got this.

FEAR

OF FAILURE AND SUCCESS

"Everything you want is on the other side of fear."

-Jack Canfield

FEATURING:
KRISTEN THOMPSON
ESTEE ROE
KRISTY KEUS
MICHELLE B. VAZQUEZ

Thee is something about taking action that is equal parts terrifying and thrilling. When I was in the initial brainstorming stages of this book, I was flooded with excitement and passion. I had a message to share, an amazing team of talented writers, and a supportive publisher—I was going after my dreams and felt unstoppable. But life has a funny way of keeping you humble and it was no sooner that I opened my laptop to start on my chapter that the excitement drained out of me and I found myself flooded with the feelings I have worked so hard to rid myself of—self-doubt and anxiety. All of a sudden, the enthusiasm I once felt had faded into the background, becoming almost impossible to hear amidst the screaming in my head.

What if you fail?

And I was not alone. Many of the authors grappled with fear and self-doubt when approaching this book, questioning how on earth they could write about tackling fear when they didn't feel like they had overcome it themselves? How do you encourage others to explore and combat their fears while you still struggle with your own every day?

It seemed while we all had experienced and coped with fear differently, fear of failure was the one thing to which each of us could relate. Whether we feared disappointing ourselves or others, feared success, or just felt we were undeserving of this opportunity, there was a commonality there. We were unified by the negative voices in our heads and our desire to quiet them and go after our dreams anyway. As we plowed through with our writing, it became apparent that the fear doesn't necessarily ever go away. Whether following your dreams or sitting on the sidelines, you will feel afraid at times. The trick is to let yourself feel afraid, acknowledge the fear, and do it anyway. Allow the fear to crack you open, but not break you down.

The chapters in this next section will encourage and inspire you to do just that—to not shy away from fear, but to turn towards it. To face and explore the fears we have around imposter syndrome, rejection, or failure, and to move forward anyway, in spite of them. Fear isn't going anywhere, but we can choose to have awareness, offer ourselves some understanding and grace, and give ourselves a little push. After all, as the popular adage says, *"In the end, we will only regret the chances we didn't take . . ."*

CHAPTER ELEVEN

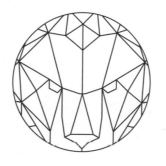

UNMASKING THE IMPOSTER WITHIN

"I want to learn to take the advice I bestow upon my children and grant myself permission to be just who I am, with my successes, failures, and everything in between."

Kristen Thompson

ig: @kristenthomps | li: Kristen Thompson
t: @KristenThom

Kristen Thompson

Kristen Thompson is a journalist, blogger, and communications specialist who resides in Kelowna, British Columbia. She's always been eager to learn more about the world around her, which is what drew her to journalism and what fuelled her desire to move to new places throughout her adulthood. That sense of curiosity pulled her out west after high school, called her to Japan after university, and eventually brought her back to Canada, where she pursued her writing career in Vancouver, Toronto, and Kelowna. Curiosity has driven her career and her many moves, but fear has been a nagging voice in the background, quietly telling her she "can't" or "shouldn't." Now that Kristen is a mother of two little girls, she is passionate about exploring the concept of fear that has held her back since childhood, so she can help her own children meet their fears head-on with confidence and resolve. She's excited to share her story with others, and join other women and writers to unpack the various ways fear grips us, and how we might be able to leave it behind.

F ear . . . the title of my document lurked at the top of the page, a single white word floating in the middle of a blue bar. Four letters without punctuation or italics: Fear. I stared at it as if to conjure the inspiration of what to write, and the word stared back, offering nothing but silence.

My cursor blinked on the empty page like a metronome: Think. Think. Think. Write. Write. Write.

"Thinking" and "writing" are what I do for a living. In some ways, they're two of the first things I was ever really good at. But then again, "good" is subjective, so when I say I was "good" at thinking and "good" at writing, what that actually means is that I met or surpassed expectations, and as such, was dubbed "good."

Being "good" at writing is what brings me here, to the blank page, the metronome cursor, and the stand-off with the title of my document, in which I am to write about fear and how it's impacted my life.

If you were to poll friends, family, and colleagues, they would likely say that I would be "good" at writing on this topic, not because I'm an expert in fear, per se, but because I'm "good" at writing. Good writers know what to say and how to say it, and therein is my hang-up—therein is the reason for the blank page. People expect me to be good at this, and so I doubt myself, and I falter.

Here's a secret you should know about me early on: I am perpetually bracing for the moment that I let people down. Or, more specifically, for the moment that I show them I'm not nearly as worthy as they think—the moment they realize I fooled them. We call it imposter syndrome. We call it self-sabotage. We call it insecurity. I call it my fear of being *found out*.

145

I don't know how long this fear has plagued me, but I can trace it back to my earliest memories. Was it the experience of every little girl growing up in a loving, middle-class family in the 80s and 90s to feel unsure of herself, afraid of making a fool, terrified of standing out? Maybe. Probably. But my fear was wrapped up in a messy knot of expectations from my teachers and parents.

The next question, of course, is this: were those expectations placed on me, or did I place them on myself? Which came first, the chicken or the egg? Or did both materialize at the same time, so there's no way to differentiate between the cause and the effect?

One of my earliest memories involves sitting cross-legged on the floor in my grandparents' living room, frantically scratching away at a "mistake" I had made on a coloring page featuring a flamingo. I had drawn outside of the lines, or had chosen the wrong shade of pink, or both. I remember using a butter knife in an attempt to peel away the wax of the crayon, sobbing, as my grandmother stood in the doorway trying to explain that you can't erase crayon, while my grandfather assured me the picture was, indeed, a masterpiece.

Just minutes earlier, they had been seated in matching armchairs watching me work, passing observations back and forth regarding how *good* I was at coloring. It's the type of praise adults often bestow upon children whether or not that child is actually good at that activity. But I took their praise seriously, and the moment I had been labeled "talented," I felt a profound need to live up to their opinion.

I had been described as talented at drawing from an early age; I suppose adults compared me to my peers. And while I enjoyed basking in my classmates' amazement—"She's so *good* at that! I wish I could draw like *her*!"—the praise, especially when it came from adults, also left me feeling vulnerable and exposed, rather than proud and self-assured. I wanted to do well and please, but I also wanted to fly under the radar because I worried: what if I drew outside the lines? What if my shading was off? What if I took on a subject that was too challenging? I was terrified of underperforming and disappointing. I was terrified of the day that the praise fell silent.

As I navigated these complicated feelings in school, I also stumbled upon another knack, this time for language and writing. When I put pen to paper I was able to articulate myself eloquently. This was true with storytelling in general: public speaking and presentations, book reports and essays, and any situation in which I had to express myself carefully and thoughtfully. These skills came naturally to me, in the same way that math or science may come naturally to another child.

In retrospect, I'm glad I sailed comfortably through assignments, essays, and tests. But the ease with which I earned my grades didn't prevent me from fretting endlessly over what would happen if I stumbled on my next assignment. I began to convince myself that my successes—rather than the occasional missteps—were the flukes. And with every well-received writing assignment, art project, or speech, I grew more and more convinced I was somehow conning my way through the system.

When I was fourteen, I received a letter in the mail welcoming me into a high school for the arts. I remember that letter well, and I remember how proud my parents were. At the time, it felt like their dream for me, rather than my dream for myself, but they had always encouraged me to challenge myself, and I saw this acceptance letter—and an eventual education in fine arts—as a worthy challenge. And yet, I also remember my thoughts as I read those typed congratulations: *I have just taken a spot away from someone else more deserving.*

This fear of rejection left me panic-stricken in my first painting class. Whereas in elementary school I had stood out among my peers, suddenly I was surrounded by teenagers whose talents equaled mine, and, in many cases, exceeded them. The playing field had been leveled; who was I now that I was no longer the best?

At the same time, the curve of my growth as an artist began to level off. Whereas I propelled ahead of my classmates in my early school years, that talent slowed down as I entered high school, and I was no longer improving in the leaps and bounds I was used to.

I remember sitting in the living room one evening tearing apart a pencil drawing I had been working on for an assignment. It was a scene from the Stephen King book *Cujo*, in which I was depicting a snarling dog jumping toward the viewer as if it were leaping right off the page. I found both the medium (pencil) and subject (a foreshortened animal) difficult. I wasn't proud of it, but imagining those close to me criticizing the as-yet-incomplete drawing filled me with a burning and profound shame. That moment somehow validated my conviction that my successes were meant to please or appease my teachers, coaches, and family. And my art in particular was good only if it was accepted by those people. There was no room to stumble and learn. There was no room to get it wrong.

So day in and day out, surrounded by dozens of talented teenagers, I would hide in the back of the room with my canvas turned away from the class, afraid to show my peers, teachers, and parents that I was the weakest link.

As I grew older, this self-doubt jumped from academia to horseback riding—the other activity for which I seemed to have a talent. In the early years, riding brought me immeasurable joy. Bonding with a beautiful animal and feeling the wind rush past you as you gallop is indescribable. As I got better and began winning competitions, I would hear coaches turn to their own students and say: "That's how I want *you* to do it"; that's when a new kind of joy emerged—the joy of success.

But as I became more competitive and the stakes grew, I felt a sense of obligation to the people who had invested in me—with either their money or their time—to go all the way. I felt like if I wasn't winning, if I wasn't working toward the penultimate success in my sport, then I was letting everyone down, and it had all been for nothing. I began to lose sight of what brought me joy about riding and agonized over every failed attempt in the first place.

I was hard on myself as an academic, an artist, and an athlete. But also, people rooting for me on the sidelines were hard on me, too. They had come to expect a certain level of performance: certain grades, certain accolades, and certain outcomes. I don't have many memories of second-place riding ribbons or B-level essays receiving praise. Instead, I remember hearing "you did your best, and that's all that matters" after coming up short in other endeavors in which I was never expected to do well, like track-and-field, math quizzes, or swim meets.

I also have vivid memories of coming home with a grade of ninety-four percent in French class and being asked, "Where did the other six percent go?" Or, third place ribbons being tossed aside by a family member because they weren't worth keeping. "We don't need to hang on to that one," the family member would say. Perhaps it was a joke or meant to highlight how unusual it was for me to get third place, but the impact was crushing. To me, the comment was a clear message that if I wasn't winning, my other accomplishments weren't worthy; it didn't honor the experience or the challenge it took to get there.

I knew intellectually that I was good at riding, that I had a wonderful partnership with my horse, and that my hard work paid off as successes in the show ring. Yet, I was full of doubt and fear. Eventually, every ribbon that came home felt like an accident, like tripping over a finish line to end in first place.

To cover up my fear—academically, athletically, and even socially—I became an extrovert. Being outgoing was something I *worked* at, rather than something that came naturally to me. I kept my social circle large. I joined clubs and groups, signed up for school trips, and took on a leadership role in planning events like prom, or projects like the yearbook. I went to parties. . . lots of parties. As long as the world saw confidence, they would never know that self-doubt plagued me every step of the way. I would become the person people *thought* I was but secretly wasn't. I would morph into that other version of myself and *become* her.

This confidence, in some ways, became a catch-22 as I moved out and started carving out a life for myself away from home. It's what propelled me onto a plane when I was nineteen, heading toward a city across the country to attend a university I'd never been to before. That confidence brought parties to my dorm room and success in my first-year classes. The more people I added to my circle of friends, peers, and mentors, the more I had to work at keeping up this lifelong sham.

I had it in my head that I wanted to study psychology, primarily because it was a topic that interested me, and I had assumed that my interest in a subject would equate to favorable grades. I was wrong. I languished in my courses, struggling to make sense of the science behind the psychology, and barely kept my grades in the passing level.

During a trip home for Christmas, my parents and I discussed my end-of-term grades, and my father observed that perhaps I wasn't cut out for psychology. I bawled: I bawled at the failure; I bawled at the idea that I had deceived him into thinking I was intelligent; and I bawled at the thought of having to regroup, pick a new major, and start again.

He was right, of course. I wasn't cut out for psychology, or science in general. You don't have to be good at everything, and that was a hard first introduction into the reality that, in many aspects of life, I was not average—I was subpar.

At the time, I was taking elective English courses and a particular professor pulled me aside one day to ask if I was taking English as a major. When I answered in the negative, he quickly convinced me I was studying the wrong subject.

As soon as I changed majors, university life changed for me. My grades skyrocketed, professors entered my essays and writing into competitions, and I was held as an example to classmates. Even still, as I came home during subsequent Christmas and summer holidays, I felt like I wouldn't be able to live up to expectations. Now that I was doing well again, the gentle sympathy I had received from family, friends, and teachers as a psychology student had transformed back into the questioning I had known before. When I got a B-plus, I was asked why I hadn't received an A. When I received an A, I was asked why I hadn't received an A-plus. I grew resentful; I felt paranoid on the days when essays were handed back, questioning every misstep in every assignment that wasn't graded with an A-plus. On my last day of university, I came home from defending my undergraduate thesis: an epic essay I had written analyzing the role of feminism in *Gone With the Wind*, and together with my roommate, burned the paper on our little concrete balcony. I had never been so relieved to have finished something that, for all intents and purposes, I had done well in.

When I was in my mid-twenties, I landed what was, at the time, my dream job: A position as a reporter at a daily newspaper in a big city. I had been interning in the newsroom for only six weeks when the role was posted, and I reluctantly added my resume to the towering stack on my editor's desk. A week later, I had beat out all other applicants. I went home and panicked because I knew that on Monday my editor was going to find out the truth: I was mediocre at best and had fluked my way into the job.

Even though I'd ridden the bus to the newsroom every day for six weeks up until then without stress, that first day as paid staff felt terrifying because I would have to prove my worth. As an intern I had been working for free, re-writing press releases, and taking photos of dog-walk fundraisers. There was nobody to let down—until that Monday.

In the end, Monday came and went without fanfare, as have hundreds of Mondays since. I did okay on that first day, and it laid the groundwork for what is now a rewarding career in writing. But even now, all this time later, I fret over my articles and am plagued by a nagging certainty that I'm disappointing my editors. I've never received that feedback, of course, but the fear of failure is deep and I'm not sure I'll ever totally overcome it.

In some ways, it has wiggled into all aspects of my life: professional, social, and personal—this perpetual fear that if someone sees me for who I really am they won't love me anymore. Or, at the very least, they will love me less. In many ways my fear keeps me from being happy and enjoying my successes. It nags me as I lay in bed, whispering that I'm not as worthy as others, calling me a fraud. It's a lie, but there's still something convincing about its voice when the house is dark and quiet and I'm alone with my self-doubt.

Now that I have daughters of my own I often wonder how my fear manifested all those years ago, and what—if anything—I can do to make them more resilient. Is my fear one of my own making, or were the people who supported me complicit? How, as a teacher, coach, or parent, do you strike a balance between instilling confidence in a child, while showing them that perfection isn't necessarily the end game?

I now know that praise can create a huge amount of pressure. I know that approval comes with burdens and that expectations can feel crippling. I also know that confidence is less about believing you are "good" at something and more about being happy with the process: the process of learning a new skill, performing at work or in your sport, and even in having meaningful relationships. I know that those of us who are seemingly independent and strong often have battles within that nobody sees, and that the more my children see me try, stumble, brush myself off, and try again, the more they might even come to celebrate their own missteps. Because of course, those missteps are the key to growth and what makes us human. I want them to know that the people who love them will see them more for their strength and resiliency, than for their grades, awards, and income.

And more than anything, I want to learn to take the advice I bestow upon them and grant myself permission to be just who I am, with my successes, failures, and everything in between. Giving myself grace isn't something I'm "good" at—just don't tell anyone.

CHAPTER TWELVE

YOU CAN

"You have two options: give in to that feeling or use it to fuel your fire. It fueled my fire."

Estee Roe

www.esteeroe.com

ig: @estee.roe | fb: @EsteeRoe

Estee Roe

A radiographer turned stay-at-home-mom turned entrepreneur, Estee is her best self when serving and empowering others. She is a high-vibrating vessel of unconditional love, support, and guidance. Her business is centered on building confidence in others with exclusive haircare and skincare products, and also offers a path for those involved to create their own financial well-being.

She finds joy in nature, laughter, live music, quality time with friends and family, heartfelt connections, all things woo-woo, new adventures, and a stellar pair of high heels.

Estee lives in a suburb of Des Moines, Iowa, with her husband, Ryan, and two kids, Nash and London.

The easiest part of writing this chapter for me: the title—because every ounce of my being believes you can. Those two words speak to me. As a mother of two little humans, I am forever telling them to intentionally get uncomfortable. It's scary. It makes you nauseous, your heart races, and if it's real good, you might sweat. Just keep going.

It took me many years and a stack of personal development books to gain this perspective. In that growth journey, I realized I have two fears that stem all the way back to childhood: failure and rejection. I grew up in small-town Iowa with loving parents and three younger siblings. My father was a truck driver and owned a livestock-hauling company. My mother stayed at home and helped with the business. In my second-grade year, we open-enrolled into another school district but did not physically relocate. We still had our home and my dad's business in our original locale. When I look back, I cannot believe the turmoil that ensued. What started out as a positive attempt at whole-grade sharing between two school districts turned into doing what was best for your family. And my parents did just that. Consequently, they lost friendships, business deals, and worst of all, respect. I will never forget running into friends from my old school. No one said, "Hi, how are you?" But rather, they looked away as we passed. Whether at the park, a ball game, the grocery store, library, or gas station, years of this would follow because we still lived in our same small town. It's difficult to understand as a young child—going from being accepted to completely rejected over this one decision. It was crushing. As my mother says, "It was just lights out." Over the years, I have been told several reasons as to why this happened. A common thread was that our family was viewed as not being loyal to our community and that the school district we open enrolled to would receive monetary benefit from our transfer. Yes, it was an unfortunate time, but it helped shape me into the women I am today. It gave me a reason to dig deeper into who I truly am and learn that overcoming fear is what leads to personal growth.

I met my husband, Ryan, when I was twenty-four and by twenty-eight, we were married with two children: our son, Nash, and daughter, London—two complete opposites all the way down to their respective pregnancies and delivery. Nash came into this world and out went my mobility. I developed a femoral neuropathy after delivery that left me unable to walk or carry him. It was an incredibly challenging time for us. I was prescribed intense physical therapy four days a week. The physical therapist would hold and comfort Nash during my appointments—an odd feeling to watch as a new mother. I had to concentrate on every step I took or I would fall down, even while using my walker (complete with tennis balls). I remember belly-laughing at a joke with my sister, forgetting for a split second my reality, and falling behind my desk. It was a time I will never forget. I even learned how to drive with my left foot! I made huge strides—finally being able to walk on my own seven months later. The doctor's prognosis was one year, so this felt like the biggest achievement to me even after welcoming a new baby.

Also in that time, when Nash was nineteen days old, he stopped breathing. Watching your husband perform CPR on your new baby is something I really cannot explain. It's numbing. After extensive testing and an overnight stay, they diagnosed him as a SIDS case that was caught early. Talk about fear of failure as a mom. I let fear take over. After such a traumatic experience, the only way I knew to curb any fear-based thoughts was by gaining more control. It was only natural that I wanted nothing less for my son than rainbows and butterflies. Realistic, right? I am an organized person, but I became uber-organized: made baby food at home, videoed every "ooh" and "aww," placed all of our pictures in a perfectly-crafted scrapbook, had an over-the-top first birthday party... the list goes on. I loved seeing and hearing about all the parents who left no stone unturned. I truly admired their mad skills. My truth: it exhausted me to my core. The weight of trying to keep up with the latest, greatest thing, and the perfectionist standard I set for myself—it all became too much. Then, add another baby. After having London, I knew something had to give. I was waking up in the middle of the night with a rapid heart rate and shortness of breath. I was obsessing over obsessing. Mom-guilt is a real thing. Insert: fear of rejection. I can still feel the anxiousness I had when I began navigating my new path of fearlessness.

As I aligned my inner-peace with an acknowledgment of my imperfections and started caring less about others' validation, I began to *do me* as a parent. By all means, it did not happen overnight and there are still moments of regression, but the thoughts of *will our kids have good memories* and *did I do everything I could with the time I had* subsided. I became focused on what mattered to me, not everyone else. I no longer worried about sign-up dates for every possible class or activity; instead, I picked one or two things and went with it. I still snapped a million pictures, videoed our daily lives, and had birthday parties. But rather than perfectly-crafted scrapbooks, well-designed home videos, and big birthday parties, I let myself off the hook. The pictures were uploaded (some were printed, others I'm still getting to), videos were left unedited and saved on a USB drive, and birthday parties were exclusively with our family.

Fast forward a few years to when we sent London to kindergarten. Having been a stay-at-home mom for almost eight years, it was admittedly nice to go through the day on my own schedule. While I wouldn't trade the years that Nash and London were at home for absolutely anything, I did love holding more than half of a thought when I was grocery shopping, that my appointments weren't scheduled around breakfast, lunch, naps, or feedings, and that I could volunteer at the school and work on an as-needed basis.

Oh yes, this brings me to my early adult life. Back to that. I graduated from college with a degree in both radiology and healthcare management and even began taking classes for my master's in healthcare administration. I loved my job. I loved the places I worked. I loved my patients and many of my relationships with co-workers turned into lifelong friendships. I was always eager for more and looked forward to growing my career in healthcare. I worked part-time when the kids were little, but that required my mother to travel for an hour to come babysit. As much as I appreciated her help and needed the adult interaction at work, it became more of a hassle than it was worth. Ryan and I brainstormed multiple ways for me to make money working from home, including stuffing envelopes or a paper route! So when the newness of not having kids at home wore off, I was ready for something to call my own.

I fell into employment at a direct sales company—my first job of that sort, I might add—somewhat by accident. I was losing my hair and wanted it back. A dear friend introduced me to a product line that corrected my hair loss, and not only that, I had several people comment on how much better it looked. I never had *bad* hair, so I found this to be surprising. That's when a light bulb went off—maybe I need to explore this as a business? So I did.

Six months into this journey, I decided I was going to "retire" from healthcare as a rad-tech and focus on my shampoo business full-time. I was incredibly nervous and scared, but it was exciting. I felt it in my bones. I did not know what it looked like or how I would do it, but I was in. All in. You can imagine Ryan's reaction when I told him I had *retired* from a secure job in healthcare to sell hair care products. Now it wouldn't be fair to say he didn't support me, but he certainly did not agree with my blind leap of faith. Ryan has a very black-and-white personality. He's a surgeon, so rationality is understandably his nature. I tend to just go all in when I get a good-yet-uncomfortable feeling and deal with all of the details later.

My new business was exciting and overwhelming at the same time. I loved the community, the emphasis on gratitude, and, most of all, I simply loved being able to work from home and get the kids on and off the bus.

It was not until I entered the direct sales world that I began to feel shifts. I was so excited to share these products that had helped me stop losing hair with every single human I knew. I learned quickly that the majority of your friends and family will support you, but not all. Some thought it was a cute thing I was doing because I was a housewife with kids now in school. Others couldn't believe I was now a *salesperson*. One of the most unsolicited statements during this time was, "Remember when you had an important job?" That one stung a little bit. I found it shocking and unexpected, and it left me feeling confused, hurt, and unsure of myself. Welcome back, rejection. Why was such an emphasis being put on what I was doing? I did my best to not let it get to me, but I'd be lying if I said I didn't wonder if they were right. Was Ryan right for thinking I was half-nuts for throwing a career out the window for shampoo? Maybe. But I will never understand why, as a woman whose spouse has a well-paying job, it can be viewed as selfish or ungrateful for wanting more. Why did his profession have to be my identity, too? I am fortunate that I do not need to work for us to make ends meet, but at the end of the day, I needed, and more importantly, I wanted something of my own.

When I dug into what I wanted my business to look like, I can see now that it took becoming uncomfortable for me to achieve my goals. I am introverted by nature and the thought of putting myself "out there" to people I did not know made my stomach flip. This was uncharted territory for me. Until this point, I worked in hospitals and clinics; I had been a team player, but now it was just me, myself, and I. I made a promise to myself that if I was going to do this, I would be as true to myself as humanly possible. What did that mean? It meant I was going to start networking and building genuine relationships with people. I had never networked before, so all those self-development books came in handy because I knew who I was, what my strengths and weaknesses were, and figured out how to put it all together. There were many times I thought it would be so much easier to go back to a steady paycheck, where I didn't have to develop trust and be vulnerable with people who had no idea who was the real me. Sure I can strike up a conversation and make small talk, but it leaves me feeling empty. I love getting to know people; I want to find out what makes them tick. I learned that while there are those who appreciate openness and honesty, there are also those who find it off-putting. I began overthinking everything I was saying. And then I thought: *Are you kidding me?! Who is this person*

I'm becoming? It was a trying time and I was in a mind game. I felt myself digressing into the people-pleaser I once was in hopes of establishing a relationship. As a child, I was shown quite clearly what can happen when you go against popular beliefs by staying true to yourself, and there was a part of me that wanted to give up. But, in a strange way, my childhood experience also gave me the grit to navigate this new path. I have been given the cold shoulder, a dismissive nod, heard people say, "Ohhh a multi-level," and have been asked, "Is that one of those pyramid schemes?" I have heard the word "no" more times in the last three years than I have in my entire life. It does not make one feel awesome, but you have two options: give in to that feeling or use it to fuel your fire. It fueled my fire.

Despite the rejection and the "no's," I have received the kindest words of support and encouragement, met incredibly inspiring women, been welcomed into communities I never knew existed, and developed the most solid relationships I have had outside of my marriage. When I sit down for coffee or lunch with someone new, it brings me so much joy. I love connecting with other women, sharing our successful (and not so successful) stories, and graciously supporting one another. Had I let those feelings of doubt, uncertainty, and insecurity get to me; had I listened to the opinions of others, and not leaped out of my comfort zone; I would not have the confidence that I have today. I had a vision of helping so many others gain back their confidence, and that kept my confidence afloat when conflict arose. Fear can cause people to shrink. There were times that I wondered if I have what it takes because I am an imperfect human. But I know that trial and error are simply a part of growing and living. I learned a new respect for the word "no." I used to cringe, doubt myself, and feel like giving up every time I heard it. Those fears are now my inner-compass and they help to push me past my emotional barriers. At the end of the day, I am proud of myself for starting something that was never on my radar and was outside my comfort zone.

Even as I wrap-up with this chapter, I know there will be more fears of failure and rejection throughout my journey. The funny thing about fear is that once you recognize it, it can be incredibly empowering. I am now at a place where I welcome fear and uncomfortable situations because I know that is how I will continue to grow and lead by example for my kids, and maybe for you, too. Does my stomach flip? Does my heart race? Do I sweat? Absolutely! But I know I can use this fearful energy as fuel to get through anything. You can, too.

CHAPTER THIRTEEN

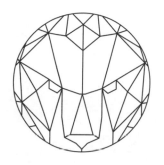

YOU CAN DO HARD F***IN' THINGS

"Now, instead of shutting down when fear boils to the surface, the nerves are calmed momentarily and are taken as adrenaline to lead."

Kristy Keus

ig: @kristykeus | fb: @KristyKeus

Kristy Keus

Kristy Keus has a huge heart and a passion for helping everyone around her; people are inspired by and drawn to her authenticity and zest for life. Faith, family, friends, and fitness—this is what Kristy holds dear to her heart.

Kristy left home at fifteen to begin her adult life; she completed high school via distance education and started working. Married at seventeen, she had two children by the age of twenty-one—she felt like she was en route to the successful family life she desired. Aching for a little more, she began her career as a fitness professional.

As a trainer, Kristy felt on top of the world, feeding off the energy she shared with her clients. This carried into her home life, allowing her to be the best mom, like she'd always dreamed to be. When Kristy owned an indoor cycling studio, teaching classes every evening, she came home refreshed, rejuvenated, and alive!

After their third child was born, Kristy's family moved to a bigger city to reach further successes; she always stares fear in the eye and makes sure she comes out ahead.

She reminds us all to stop being afraid of what could go wrong and to instead focus on being excited for what could go *right*!

As I considered the many times I had experienced fear and overcome it, which gave me the self-proclaimed authority to even consider writing about such a topic, I realized I still face fear every day. The difference is that now I can acknowledge and work my way through it.

We all grow up eventually, and sometimes we think that growing up is synonymous with overcoming fear.

It. Is. Not.

We must choose to step up to our fears head-on and beat them down. This can happen at any age. Some of us are bold enough to fight it in our youth, while others let fear control them for decades before becoming strong and courageous enough to overcome it.

If we let fear control us, we will not grow up to the best of our God-given potential. With every step we take to squash our fears, we grow into a more capable human being, able to take on the world. To me, this means I can be a better person—an amazing mom, a loving partner, a caring sister and daughter, a trustworthy and fun best friend, a responsible and generous member of society, and a kick-ass personal trainer!

We all have our childhood stories that shape us into who we are today.

I grew up with parents who were separated, which is not unusual this day and age, but was still traumatic to a young perfectionist who perpetually felt incapable of doing things right, who felt that she had to make everyone happy. As the older sibling, I felt like the go-between for my parents, who didn't communicate, and I was always left feeling like I wasn't good enough—like I was going to let someone down. I was always carrying others' burdens.

Having a mother that dealt with depression and alcoholism while working hard to give us the best life she could left

169

little time for the things I truly needed—quality time together and connection. My workaholic father also had little time for my sister and me, and this behavior continues even to this day, adding to a terrible feeling of diminished self-esteem. When we did see him, he made us feel inadequate, which hurt even though he did it unintentionally. We were never able to live up to his expectations or do what he wanted us to. I recall a water-skiing attempt where I couldn't get up on my skis; his frustration haunts me to this day.

My fear of not being good enough stems from these "minor" traumas and developed into many years of people-pleasing—doing whatever it took to feel accepted and loved, even sacrificing my true self.

Now that I am a parent, I understand the difficulties of raising tiny humans, and I wish I had realized sooner how impactful those early years are.

My teen years continued on the same path. I feared being what I often felt I truly was: worthless. I turned to alcohol and drugs early, trying to escape that awful feeling. The perfectionist in me would not let the situation get out of control, because that would also have been a failure. So, I drank just enough to take the edge off; smoked just enough to keep up with the "cool kids"; spent just enough time with the wrong crowd, who made me feel adored for my looks, but left my soul feeling empty; cried and felt sorry for myself just enough to light a fire under my butt to be better than all of this.

Then, when I was fifteen, I met a boy. An older boy who "loved" me and told me he would take care of me—he'd make all my dreams come true. Fearing I was not strong enough to do anything on my own, I believed him. I thought I was being brave, choosing to leave home with him and start living for myself. Looking back now, I am not sure it was bravery that made me leap into adulthood, or if it was the fear that I would lose his love. All I knew at the time was that I would do anything to make this love last forever. I was never going to leave this man no matter what. We would beat the odds and make it! So, we began our life together when we moved twelve hours away from friends and family with nothing more than what fit in our vehicle and the little bit of cash two teenagers could have.

From as early as I can remember, I was always mothering my younger cousins, the other kids at daycare, and any child who looked up to me. I was the older kid who loved teaching—okay, maybe bossing around—those adorable little people. I especially loved choreographing dances. At the daycare I attended, I made sure all the kids loved dancing with me.

Having a deep desire to help others, I thought of becoming a teacher when I grew up. I thought I could reach many people this way. I was a perfectionist; I made sure to have the best grades growing up and tried my damnedest to make sure I was liked by all. The one thing holding me back from taking this route was the even deeper desire to become a mother as soon as possible. So instead of going on a five-year university path to becoming a teacher, my husband and I chose to start our family early.

I was nineteen years old, almost two years into my marriage, when I was blessed with a beautiful baby girl. From the moment I laid eyes on her, I didn't ever want to leave her side. She was perfect and I was in my glory. Feeling like I was doing a boss job of parenting my perfect little angel, I knew I was ready to take on something more. Not wanting to leave her with anyone—because, let's face it, I was the *best* thing for her and nobody would take care of her like me—I had to find something that I could do *with* her.

I loved being active and had to find a way to bounce back after having a baby, but our little family was near the poverty line. Being a resourceful person, I decided that since I couldn't afford to take a fitness class, I would become an instructor. It fit everything I needed: the ability to teach and help others, keep me in shape, earn money for my family, and keep my baby with me for most of my day.

As soon as we saved up enough money, I enrolled in a self-study fitness theory course. I quickly crushed it and nailed my exams. For the next step in becoming certified, I had to take an in-class course on evenings and weekends. This was painful for me, though my baby girl and her daddy were just fine at home. It was for the greater good, so I accepted what I had to do.

The course was run at the local YMCA. The instructor was perfect; I aced my tests! When it was almost over, I started to get cold feet. The realization that I had to stand up in front of people hit me; these were people who, in my mind, were much better than me. I began feeling unworthy and unable to continue. I was fear-struck and wanted to quit. I called the instructor and told her I could not complete the course, that I wouldn't be back the next day. Feelings of being incapable filled my body to the point where I couldn't focus on anything other than giving up.

The words she spoke to me are still in my head: "You can do this. I see your potential and you will be great!" My mind was blown. I had never heard that before. A parent or teacher may have said those words, but I had never *heard* it.

Those words motivated me, inspired me, and gave me the courage I needed to walk through my fear in that moment. I went to my class the next day, scared out of my mind of embarrassing myself. The fear I grew up with filled my entire being as I took front and center, leading my peers through an exercise program. *Who the heck was I to be teaching them?* I was terrified of making a fool of myself. But I did it—I did the hard thing and came through stronger on the other side!

I am forever grateful to my teacher for giving me life-changing encouragement. I had never had someone tell me I make good choices; I constantly second-guessed myself. I had no confidence at all! That little ounce of courage led me to where I am today—fifteen years on and still instructing.

Even though the nerves still flood me before each class, I breathe in knowing I will deliver my best. In my classes, I give my spirit and my passion to everyone who attends. It is a labor of love. But, even though many people in my classes respond with words of affirmation, I always have a hard time hearing (and especially believing) that anyone could appreciate me and enjoy what I have to offer. I had done it! The times I felt happiest was when I was training—when I could be *this* me. I was confident! I had faced my fear and won the battle. I worked with my fear and became a great trainer. Now, instead of shutting down when fear boiled to the surface, I had learned to momentarily calm my nerves and turn them into the adrenaline I needed to lead. I was fearless.

But was it me who was fearless? Or was it just the trainer version of myself?

In the rest of my life, this "other me" needed some help.

I was hit with a heavy, unexpected blow, after being "convinced" everything was okay.

I was living with this pit in my stomach telling me that something was wrong, that my marriage was failing. I had wanted out of my marriage for years, but I feared leaving and being deemed a failure. My husband reassured me that we were good. So, why was I feeling this way? He refused counseling because "we were good." I knew that was a lie, so why did he keep saying it? I constantly reminded myself that I had to make this "fairy tale" work. How could I be a better wife? Was there something wrong with me? Why didn't I just leave? My self-doubt was at an all-time high, but I struggled with my internal debate: *Should I stay in a marriage that isn't working? Or should I leave it?* I was afraid of making the wrong decision, so I stayed put—I didn't want to cause waves. My childhood fears reared their ugly head when I wasn't rocking my Confident Trainer persona.

And then it happened: he left me. He left me?! The choice was made for me. My fear took away my freedom to make a choice, one that I knew in my gut was right. I didn't trust my intuition, so it slapped me upside the head. But, I was free. Hallelujah! But, I was afraid. After all the reassurance and promises, my ego took a huge blow—so did my self-esteem, courage, and trust.

I had given my teenage years and my entire adult life to him. We raised children and tried to make a life together. Now what?

I felt completely worthless and incapable of making any decision for myself. Years of self-doubt and false reassurance will do that to a person.

The fight against him. The fight for the kids. The fight to survive—physically, mentally, financially. I didn't know how to do it. I didn't have a soul to help me. I had never told anyone about our troubles at home or my low self-esteem. I couldn't let anyone know I was less than perfect. I couldn't even wrangle my thoughts into words. Fear was at the forefront of every choice I was faced with.

I was afraid to leave all that I had known. Afraid that I would not be accepted. Afraid that I wasn't enough for anyone—even myself. For twenty years I had lived behind this man and within my marriage. After he left, I realized I had to learn to care for myself to care for my children. *Why was this happening? Where should I start?*

I chose the task with the closest deadline—I could only take a glimpse into the planning of my future. I was pulled in so many directions and constantly felt rushed. My first obstacle was to earn an income to keep myself and my children safe. Check. This was surprisingly simpler than my fearful mind had expected; I never gave myself enough credit for how personable I was, and how my strong work ethic showed to those around me. As I learned to survive on my own, my self-esteem grew. Of course, each day I feared not being good enough—at my job, at parenting, at life. So, I continued taking on more and more until I lost myself in tasks and didn't have time to think about the dark clouds over my head or the pain in my heart.

I felt a shift. At thirty-five, I was finally free to make my own choices. Free of the judgment from others. I decided to take a trip with my friend Jade, and for this, I will be forever grateful. I joined her at a retreat where we released our pain and learned to open up to start a new path. This trip changed my life.

I held my pain and fear inside, vibrating and trying to keep a brave face, as we worked through an exercise of stomping to release our pain. What if I did let go? What if I did release my anger and pain? Would I be weak? I wouldn't be strong enough. The raging fire inside me was keeping me alive. Suddenly, I felt my feet stamping the ground in frustration, then I let out a quiet scream. The pain in my soul was overbearing and I unleashed it in a toddler-like tantrum. I was fighting myself—*hold it in! No, release it!*

The tension built up until I could no longer hold back; it was orgasmic, in a sense, now that I look back. The explosion of tears and emotion was so intense that I was left breathless, gasping for air. I left silently, slinking into a hot shower to dissolve the intensity I had felt. I used a breathing exercise to slow my heart and focus my thoughts. Lights out.

Seven solid hours later, I awoke feeling like a weight had been lifted. I wondered, *what the hell just happened?*

What happened? What did I learn? I learned that I can do, and had already overcome, hard fucking things!

I knew it wasn't over—it wasn't like my fear was screamed away—but now I knew I could make it through. Next time I felt my fear and pain bottling up, I would be able to recognize and release it sooner, turning it into a distant memory.

I must work hard every damn day, reminding myself that I am more than enough! I have been misinformed by others my whole life; I won't judge a child for misspelling a word they never heard, why should I blame myself for things I have yet to try? We do not know what we do not know. We learn, we grow, we make better choices.

I am not failing. I am trying and building a better self.

I am not afraid. I can do hard things and I can overcome whatever is set before me.

I am safe when I choose me and I shall no longer live as a self-conscious, fearful, low-self-esteemed people pleaser.

I recommend graciously accepting the responsibility of being the voice in the back of your mind telling you that *you can do the hard thing!* Learn the thing, conquer it, and reach your goals. Your fear wants to win, to hold you back. You are stronger than that fear. That desire to live your best life is within your reach—go for it.

"F-E-A-R has two meanings:
Forget Everything And Run or
Face Everything And Rise.
The choice is yours."

-Zig Ziglar

CHAPTER FOURTEEN

FEAR WILL NOT STEAL MY THUNDER!

"Only then will you start gaining territory in the confidence department of your brain, which will then begin a ripple effect of transformation."

Michelle B. Vazquez

www.perfectlycraftedme.com

ig: @Perfectly_crafted_me | fb: @perfectlycraftedme

Michelle B. Vazquez

Michelle B. Vazquez is a wife and a mother of three girls. She is an entrepreneur, business owner, and blogger. Michelle is the founder of the *Perfectly Crafted Me* blog, where she shares her passions, faith, and advice for how to live to your fullest potential. She is an advocate for the sanctity of life and has organized charity concerts to build up and sustain the lives of children with disabilities in Guatemala. She is best known for her passionate speaking and empowering messages on living out one's purpose to become the person God created you to be. She created a social media community called *Rise Up*, in which she delivers content to create a Christian growth-mindset to surpass limiting beliefs and help others reach their goals. One of her biggest dreams is to create a non-profit organization to provide resources to Hispanic and African-American girls to help them reach their full potential.

Michelle has a bachelor's degree in chemistry from the University of Puerto Rico and is now pursuing a master's degree in art therapy and mental health. Her passion for helping others is her focus. Michelle's education and life experiences have provided many opportunities for her to give back to others and to further her desire to be the salt and light of the earth.

"Being aware of your fear is smart. Overcoming it is the mark of a successful person."

-Seth Godin

Fear: one of the strongest human emotions there is. Every human, at some point in their lives, has to battle fear. Fear can create wars, fear can create peace, fear can empower you or limit you. Fear starts in our mind but can be felt all over our bodies, crippling us, destroying our will to move forward. We cannot be fearless by nature, but we can dig within ourselves and not let fear have the final say. Believing that we can live a life without experiencing fear is just as big of a lie as saying that our planet is flat. We all experience fear! It is part of our innate defense mechanism for survival. The purpose of fear is to warn us of danger; it is how we survive. However, fear becomes a limiting emotion when we allow it to take over our thoughts, limiting our ability to reach our goals. Yep! Fear is cancer to our goals! We stop pursuing our dreams because we start becoming fearful. We begin creating self-doubt, thinking about the "what-ifs," and all of a sudden it consumes our momentum and our desire to move forward, putting us in a standstill that then leads to anxiety and deception. We get stuck in a rut with an attitude of self-pity that does not serve us.

This was me—stuck in self-pity, consumed by self-doubt and fearful of what others may say about all I did and all I was. I never understood why my desire to please others was so strong, even when it was damaging to my self-esteem. I let fear sabotage my future, like a bad tattoo on my face. Countless times it stopped me from taking the first step toward pursuing my dreams. It took me many years and many "pity parties" to stop feeling sorry for myself and face this dream-crushing troll

181

face-to-face. I had to look back and find where this all started. Everything has a beginning. Many of our self-inflicted fearful thoughts are planted in our subconscious mind long before they surface. So, I went hunting through my memories for all the relevant life experiences to understand why I was so freaking scared of rejection. Why was I limiting myself to the point of silencing my voice and not sharing my story with others? I had a deep conviction that I was meant for much more. My introverted personality is not an excuse for not becoming the person I was meant to be. I was tired of stopping myself from wanting more from life.

Once I made the terrifying decision to face my fear of rejection, all sorts of emotions started to come forward. Everything from anger to sadness was emerging. I felt immense anger toward myself for allowing years to pass by being stuck in a standstill, not pursuing my dreams. How could I think so little of myself to not become the person God intended me to be? Here is the thing: I knew what I was capable of doing! I had a message to share with the world, but how on earth would I make an impact if my fear of rejection was getting in the way? Fear can be such a troublemaker because it transforms into an excuse we sell to ourselves to just settle. We were not meant to settle if we desire more from life. It's not okay to settle when you are capable of more. It's not okay to settle if you know you can change the world for the better. Fear can feed you lies that poison you to believe you can't.

Before you can overcome your fears, you must face them, you must adopt courage and decide that fear will no longer limit you or define you. You will never prove to yourself what you're capable of if you let the emotions that arise from fear control your life. It's *okay* to be fearful. What is not okay is to settle for a life of under-achievements because it is easier to let fear take over. There is no easy way out of it, the only way to overcome fear is to push through, like a quarterback during the Super Bowl. Yep, I now face my fears as if I am playing football. I am the quarterback of my life and the football in my hands is my dream. I need to get that ball to the end zone, but I will face fierce opposition in the trajectory. This is a daunting prospect, but I will use the emotions that fear creates within me to propel me through that field of life and get there no matter what. When you train your brain to move forward despite fear, you are reprogramming your mind to accept fear without compromising your ability to go for your dreams.

It took me years to uncover the life experiences that scarred me at a deep level, the ones that made me fearful of rejection. I remember having my first face-to-face with the fear of rejection while I was in college. I was competing to be part of a team of students who would travel out of state to present research in a chemistry expo. I was so excited about this opportunity—I worked day and night to deliver the best speech. I am sure that was when my caffeine addiction started, and coffee became my best friend. I knew that the only way I would be able to get selected was to deliver an outstanding presentation. When the day arrived, something happened—I froze.

I was like a statue; fear took over my body and mind like ants over sugar. I arrived at the auditorium and started to see my competition, which is when I began to hear my peers commenting. All of a sudden, I began to put myself down, degrading my work, and comparing myself to others. I was flooded with thoughts like: *You are not good enough, you do not belong here, you will be laughed at* . . . My mind went into anxiety-mode, filled with fearful thoughts that controlled me, and I ran. I stopped myself from participating, from allowing myself to compete, and from possibly winning. I closed myself off from gaining new experiences, which sucks big time.

What still haunts me to this day is that I know I had a killer presentation and that I had as good a chance as anybody in that auditorium. Again, I allowed fear to have the final say. I remember crying with shame in my dorm room for days. I went from being fearful to being filled with anger and disappointment. I felt embarrassed about how fear led me to act. The self-pity I started to experience was so intense that I got sick of feeling limited. What is worse, I was limited not by external forces or circumstances, but by *me*, which is pretty lousy. However, it was then that I had matured enough to understand what fear would do to my life if I let it take over. Something had to change! Some internal work needed to be done to transform my mindset from playing it safe to moving forward, despite being afraid. I started to ask myself: *What made me so fearful? Why was I experiencing stomach-aching anxiety?*

I began to search for an antidote to my fears. I remember getting better at redirecting my mind and getting through uncomfortable situations. Still, I could not live *fearlessly*, and that bothered me. I was scared to the core to be rejected and not accepted; I was afraid that I was not good enough to be the person I wanted to be. But why? How did I get this way? What went wrong? And more specifically, how do I fix it? This is a challenge because we can be so critical and hard on ourselves that we degrade and undervalue our good qualities, virtues, and talents to the point of believing we are worthless.

It was then that I started to search for answers. I wanted to be different, I tried to reprogram my brain to pass by the fear. I decided that I was not going to let fear take away my life experiences and my dreams. Most importantly, I did not want fear to stop me from being the person I knew in my heart I was created to be. I wanted to go through life being fair to myself.

I started a journey to defeat fear, which led me to uncover the reality of my fear. During this process, many life experiences resurfaced, and I questioned their traumatic effect on me. Our life experiences help mold our self-esteem, as well as our mindsets, and are capable of defining our future, for better or worse. We all process life events differently, and by no means does that make us weak or "less than." It just means we are human. We are what we believe ourselves to be. For years, I lived in self-doubt and unworthiness, making myself think I could not do X, Y, or Z. Hiding behind the belief that I was simply an introverted person, I was convinced that I could not achieve my dreams. The reality was that I was so afraid of being rejected that I chose not to put myself in the spotlight, Often thinking I would be humiliated to the point where I would die of embarrassment, or, even worse, shame my family. That fear became so strong that I had nightmares every time I had to do something that would bring me attention. So, I played it safe every single time! I never overdid anything to the point where all the focus was on me. I was always a follower and never a leader. The constant negative thoughts led to a morbidly obsessed brain full of negativity. Yep, I had to shed bad habits and start feeding my mind a different mojo.

I started training my brain by practicing self-love and guarding every single thought that I let in like a defensive tackle during the Super Bowl. Once you truly decide to change, you embrace the journey. No storm can be strong enough to derail you. Yes, the storm can shake you and bring you down momentarily, stealing your motivation and even making you question your self-worth, but if you can see the person you strive to be and the impact you are going to make, you persevere. The storm will not stop you; it can only delay you for a moment. You are responsible for becoming the person you want to be—you, and only you, can do it. However, it was not until I had made peace with the fact that becoming fearless was the wrong goal when I started to reach transformational milestones. Trying to become fearless is more limiting than fear itself. The fact that I could not fearlessly pursue my goals gave me even more anxiety and depression. I thought that the answer to my problem was to eradicate fear and conquer the world. What a misconception I had about fear! It's like going to war without truly understanding your enemy and having the wrong battlefield strategy. Surprisingly enough, I managed to survive during my encounters with fear. Still, I was not thriving or achieving as much as I knew I was capable of. It was in January 2010 when I was able to confront fear as I have never done before.

I had a case of optic neuritis, which caused my optic nerve to swell so severely that I was blind for a couple of months. It was one of the scariest times of my life. However, that temporary blindness led me to understand that fear is not something we can erase from our bank of human emotions. There is value in fear! Fear can teach invaluable lessons. My blindness made me fearful of the things I was no longer able to see, but it reminded me of all the things I had not done or tried. For example, I had always wanted to change careers and become a teacher but was fearful of taking the first step and getting my teaching certification. I also wanted to paint more, but always put it off because I was too critical of myself. Funny how it wasn't so much the big things that bothered me, like the fact that I've never taken a vacation to an exotic place. Instead, it was all the little, reachable things that I could have done but did not do because I feared not being good enough, creative enough, or committed enough. If my sight did not come back, I would have to live with the fact that I did not embrace the life I was created to live because I was scared of the "what-ifs." The whole point is that it is impossible to live fearlessly and if you focus all your energy on trying to become fearless, you will live for fear because you will be constantly trying to run from it. We need to live every day open to the possibility of experiencing fear, but understand that we have full control over our will to surpass it. We can control it by lowering the noise it makes in our heads. It's your choice how you lower or mute its noise. I have found that the best way of doing so is by moving forward and encouraging myself to move past it.

It's okay to be fearful; it is okay to acknowledge fear. It is from fear that we cultivate the strength to rise up, to achieve more, to love deeper, to appreciate the now, to value opportunity, to be grateful for what we have. It is in fear that we can value our self-worth, and most importantly, it teaches us to live by faith. We are not weaker or "less than" because we feel fear! Now put yourself in front of fear and say, *Hey pal, move aside, I'm in charge. You will not steal my thunder!*

Fear can be molded into courage when you tackle the things that scare you: start reprogramming your brain to think, *Hey, that was scary, but nobody died and I did quite well! I can do this again.* Only then will you start gaining territory in the confidence department of your brain, which will then begin a ripple effect of transformation. Imagine yourself without the limiting beliefs that fear brings into your life. What things will you accomplish that are important to you? Will you start to see your reflection in the mirror differently and gather the armor to battle it in the field of life?

Fear will continue to test me, and it's okay because I will continue to transform it into lessons of gratitude. Fear will continue to test you as well. Don't hide from it—face it, embrace it, and learn from it. I accepted fear as part of being human, but I will no longer let it take over my life or deprive me of the future I want to have. Understand that fear feeds itself from our thoughts and then feed your mind the thoughts that will disarm it. Don't ever let fear steal your thunder! Be kind, be grateful, and give yourself a fighting chance because you are worthy and perfectly created.

ACKNOWLEDGMENTS

"Thank you to those who have been part of my journey. To my parents, teachers, and coaches for supporting me. And to Ben, it is with your love that I have been able to share my story."

-Haily Kortekaas

"For my parents who are my guardian angels, my husband who is the yin to my yang, and my children who are my forever teachers. I love you with all of my being."

-Lisa Kern

"To my mom and my siblings for being there for me during my toughest moments; and to Karl, I continue to be in awe of your unconditional love, support, and rock-solid patience."

-Ang (Angelika McKeen)

"Thank you to my sweet husband for loving me through all of the stages, seasons, and appointments, and continuing to grow with me."

-Betsy Grinder

"For my boys, Davin and Max—my greatest teachers, my greatest loves. Thank you for showing me that I was capable of more, for inspiring me to be a better person, and for always making me laugh."

-Christine Esovoloff

"Thank you to everybody and everything that has led me to now. My family, my teachers, my amazing partner Richard, and my darling daughter Aria. I love you."

-Andrea Kelly

"With love and gratitude to the memory of Mom and Dad; to the family that I am blessed to call mine; and to my friends who shared their wisdom, strength, and love when I needed it most."

-Lorene Hughes

"Thank you to my incredibly supportive parents, my husband, and our little boy. Thanks to my girlfriends who inspire me and let me gab, especially about writing, such as my writer-friends Kristen and Lucie, and my sister Lisa."

-Rebecca Juetten

"With love to my children, Aly and Davis. Thank you for making me brave, and for supporting me when I am not."

-Sharon Hughes-Geekie (a.k.a. Mom)

"My parents and grandparents—examples of strength in the face of life challenges; my sister—if we could do-over, I'd be your twin; my daughters—you chose me. I love you!"

-Lisa Poznikoff

"Thank you to my parents, who above all else taught me resiliency, strength, and courage, who have always pushed me to be the best version of myself, and have shown me the gift of unconditional love."

-Kristen Thompson

"Thank you, Dad, for the rock; Mom for the roll; Ryan for unending patience, love, and support; my kids for simply being themselves; and all of those who have influenced me along the way."

-Estee Roe

"To my children, Bella, Jaleb, and Kalla for gracing me with their love and laughter, and choosing me to be their mom. I will be forever grateful for the fabulous people in my life!"

-Kristy Keus

"I am grateful to God for giving me the experiences I have lived through to share and empower others to live their best life despite their fears. To my husband for supporting my every move. To my daughters Sarah, Elena, and Emma for reminding me that miracles are real."

-Michelle B. Vazquez

GOLDEN BRICK ROAD
PUBLISHING HOUSE

Link arms with us as we pave new paths to a better and more expansive world.

Golden Brick Road Publishing House (GBRPH) is a small, independently initiated boutique press created to provide social-innovation entrepreneurs, experts, and leaders a space in which they can develop their writing skills and content to reach existing audiences as well as new readers.

Serving an ambitious catalogue of books by individual authors, GBRPH also boasts a unique co-author program that capitalizes on the concept of "many hands make light work." GBRPH works with our authors as partners. Thanks to the value, originality, and fresh ideas we provide our readers, GBRPH books have won ten awards and are now available in bookstores across North America.

We aim to develop content that effects positive social change while empowering and educating our members to help them strengthen themselves and the services they provide to their clients.

Iconoclastic, ambitious, and set to enable social innovation, GBRPH is helping our writers/partners make cultural change one book at a time.

Inquire today at www.goldenbrickroad.pub